THE
ROSE-LOVER'S
GUIDE

MISTER LINCOLN
PP2370 © *The Conard Pyle Co.*

Roland A. Browne

THE
ROSE-LOVER'S
GUIDE

*A Practical Handbook on
Rose Growing*

Atheneum *New York*

1974

FOR EMALEE & LEOLA

Acknowledgments

I should be grossly remiss in courtesy if I failed to recognize all the assistance I have had from others in the absorbing pursuit of learning about roses.

Both as an amateur grower and as a writer on gardening, I have had frequent occasion to seek the advice of professional rose growers and hybridists. I have found them unfailingly helpful and patient. The late Gene Boerner of Jackson & Perkins corresponded with me for years, entertained me as his house guest, sent me countless new roses for testing, admitted me to many trade secrets, and answered my endless questions with good humor. The Huttons—Sidney senior, Sidney junior, and Richard, proprietors of Conard-Pyle—entertained me repeatedly on my trips to West Grove, and made available to me the patient, professional know-how of George

Ohlhus, who, like Gene Boerner, has devoted his entire life to the horticultural side of the rose industry. Dick Hutton sent me all their new roses for experimental growing in advance of their introduction. So did Mr. J. M. Story of Armstrong Nurseries and Mike Dering of the now defunct firm of Peterson and Dering. Ralph Moore, proprietor of Sequoia Nursery, Visalia, California, furnished me with much valuable information on miniature roses.

When the supervision of the then newly established Clarksville Municipal Rose Garden became one of my major preoccupations, Jackson & Perkins, Conard-Pyle, and Armstrong all contributed generously, sending dozens of their finest rose plants for the garden, to help the project become a reality. Nor have they ceased this practice: every year the garden is enriched by their generosity.

I don't know whether nice people tend to grow roses or growing roses makes people nice.

Introduction

A number of years ago I clipped a coupon from an advertisement in a gardening magazine and sent off for a dozen rose bushes. If I had known then what I have since learned about roses, I would never have bought them. The price was absurdly low, less than three dollars for the lot. I am sure now that the plants were greenhouse discards: bushes that had bloomed for several years, producing cut flowers for the market until they were all but exhausted. When they arrived, their appearance was not too reassuring. The tops were runty and shriveled, and the roots looked far too short, even to my unpracticed eye.

However, I was happy in my ignorant innocence. I planted them, the best I knew how, where they would get the morning sun, saw that they didn't lack for water, and was finally rewarded by the appearance of leaves on most of the plants; two or three died without ever putting out a shoot, but the others managed to reach an ultimate height of about two feet after what must have been a singularly gallant effort.

But I thought they were wonderful. When they finally came into bloom, I was enchanted. I particularly remember one bush—Golden Charm, I suspect—that produced a succession of clear yellow blooms that, to me, seemed so exquisite that I would squat on my heels in front of the little plant, lost in admiration, and finally cut a bloom to put in a vase and moon over all evening.

I did not then realize I had been hooked, that I was hopelessly in the toils of a new interest. I only knew that I liked that yellow rose. Since then I have seen it happen to many people: the more-or-less offhand planting of a few rose bushes, the gradual intensification of interest, the planting of more and more roses, the increasing mention of roses in daily conversation, the seeking out of others with similar interests, and the ultimate surrender to addiction.

At first I laid my new interest merely to intellectual curiosity. There were things going on in my rose bed that I could not understand. Why did some of the leaves develop ugly black spots, gradually turn yellow, and finally fall off? Why did some of the buds turn brown around the edges of the petals, refuse to open, and finally begin to wither? Why did a seemingly healthy, freshly cut cane turn brown at the end and begin to dry up? What caused some of the leaves to curl up into a tight roll like a cocoon? What was chewing away the soft parts of other leaves, leaving only the veins in a wraithlike skeleton of the original leaf? Clearly there was more to growing roses than merely planting and watering them.

When I asked other people who grew flowers what caused these various phenomena, I got a number of conflicting answers. No less conflicting was the advice on how to cure the disorders: spray with Black-Leaf 40; dust with sulfur; don't dust with sulfur; spray with Malathion; spray with lindane; spray with Bordeaux mixture; add lime to the soil; never add lime to the soil.

I resorted to reading. Books on roses were numerous. All one winter I read everything I could find, first in English, then in French, German, and Spanish. I ended up a little wiser, but not much. There seemed to be as many opinions as there were writers.

Roses cannot tolerate acid soil; add lime to produce an alkaline condition. Roses cannot tolerate alkalinity; add cow manure and humus to create a more acid condition. Prune heavily, leaving only three to four eyes on each cane. Prune as little as possible. Be sure that the bud union is planted an inch below the surface of the soil. Never bury the bud union; it should be at least two inches above ground level. Prune in the spring but not in the fall. Prune in the fall. Mound roses deeply in the fall with loose dirt. Never mound roses; to do so will cause cane canker. Never get water on the foliage; it will cause the spread of black spot. Spray your roses with a fine jet from the hose to wash dust from the leaves. Rig up overhead mist nozzles and grow your roses under constant moisture.

Clearly, somebody had to be wrong, or else roses were the most adaptable of all plants. I began to suspect the latter.

Finally I ignored most of the books and began growing roses in my own way. I won't say it is the best or the only way. All I know for sure is that I have grown some mighty handsome roses by methods that many would consider unorthodox if not downright heretical.

As my interest in growing roses increased, so too did the number of roses and rose beds. This was one of those problems that developed gradually, as a result of my reluctance to discard old bushes when I bought new ones. Finally I reached a point where I had over three hundred fifty bushes; to tend them properly would have occupied my every spare minute. I got rid of most of them, making a number of my gardening friends happy in the process, and reduced my plantings to about fifty bushes. However, the number of blooms that can be produced in a season by fifty well-tended bushes is little short of amazing. Even growing only fifty, my time was pretty well taken up, as I was also giving technical supervision to the Municipal Rose Garden in Clarksville, Tennessee—where we were then living—and the municipal garden then contained some seven hundred bushes.

One thing I have found out for sure: people everywhere like roses better than any other flower. There have been sporadic attempts (generally on the part of vested interests) to prove some other flower more popular, but it's a waste of time. I'm sure the Roman husband, when he found himself in the Latin equivalent of the doghouse, picked up a dozen roses on his way home from the Forum. Today, the rose still remains the favorite flower of the average American, just as it has been the symbol of beauty and loveliness to poets of all ages. Try substituting some other flower names and see what happens to the poetic image:

My luve is like a red, red petunia . . .
Gather ye delphiniums while ye may . . .
A nasturtium by any other name would smell as
sweet . . .

What accounts for the universal appeal and seemingly eternal popularity of the rose? Well, for one thing, it is undeniably handsome and smells wonderful. It comes in more sizes, shapes, and colors than any other flower. It has a longer blooming season than most flowers. And it will—and does—flourish nearly everywhere. You will find it from New York to California, from Florida to Montana. It is grown and loved in Alaska, Canada, Siberia, Japan, Mexico, Hawaii, Europe, South America, South Africa, Australia, New Zealand. I don't know of another flower that has been as widely introduced throughout the world, or that is as adaptable to as widely varying conditions of soil and climate.

The late Dr. J. H. Nicolas, one of the great rosarians of all time, in an effort to determine the soil needs of roses, once sent home soil samples taken from successful rose nurseries all over the world. He found, when the samples were analyzed, that there was absolutely no consistency in the acid-alkaline balance or any other soil factors. Rather, they varied from heavy clay to almost pure sand, and tested from extremely acid to extremely alkaline.

Since the rose *is* one of the most adaptable of all plants —nearly as adaptable as grass—why do many people still consider roses too difficult for them to grow and enjoy? Maybe it is because so much nonsense has been written about rose growing, because so many superstitions have been taken as fact.

Actually, roses are easier to grow than tomatoes, and nearly every gardener in America grows tomatoes and thinks nothing of it.

I have heard people state that the reason they didn't grow roses was that they couldn't afford to, that rose bushes were too expensive. Such a claim is absurd. New varieties of iris and day lilies sell for as much as thirty dollars for a single plant, while one bulb of a brand-new and really promising daffodil may bring from five hundred to fifteen hundred dollars. Don't take my word for this; merely check the catalogues of some of the more esoteric dealers in narcissi. Closer to home and to the experience of the average home owner, consider the prices asked for ornamental shrubs and trees—a skimpy little Japanese maple, scarcely knee-high to a tall duck, fifteen dollars. Yet it's a rare instance when a newly introduced named-rose variety costs as much as five dollars; and one that has been on the market for a few years—which may be superior to the new one—may go for as little as two dollars. Considering that a well-tended rose bush should last from five to ten years, and may last many years longer, and that it can be expected to bloom annually from early summer to the first hard frosts of autumn, the initial cost of even a new and rare variety of rose is inconsequential.

Take heart. Roses are *not* hard to grow.

Contents

Contents

THE
ROSE-LOVER'S
GUIDE

I

The Principal Types of Modern Roses

THE classification of America's favorite flower is most confusing. Complications arise because the classification has evolved haphazardly over several centuries and includes both the wild species and many hybrids; furthermore, classification names have been based upon several quite incompatible factors, such as the growth habit, the number of petals, the country of origin, and the blooming characteristics. I can well remember the deepening confusion that overwhelmed me when I began to study roses. I became so completely fuddled that I very nearly gave up.

Fortunately, many questions of classification are academic, and need not concern us at the present. The average rose grower need never be seriously concerned with them.

Hybrid teas, grandifloras, floribundas, and climbers are the few classifications about which you need to be thoroughly informed. The rest are lagniappe—things like miniatures and hybrid perpetuals and Bourbons and gallicas and mosses. I shall have occasion to mention some of these as may seem appropriate, and indeed, much of Chapter II is devoted to these lesser-known roses. But a knowledge of them is not necessarily essential to becoming a competent rosarian.

Hybrid Teas

When most people think of roses, the image that comes first to mind is of a hybrid tea rose: a big, upstanding bloom of fine form on a long, strong stem. The Germans sometimes have a way with words, and I think their name for the hybrid tea is much better than ours: *Edelrose*, "noble rose." An excellent name, for no flower is more regal, more aristocratic in appearance.

Many people refer to these roses as tea roses, which is a distinct misnomer. There *is* such a thing as a tea rose, but it is a quite different flower. It is a hybrid between *Rosa odorata*, a wild species whose leaves, when crushed, give off an odor like that of tea leaves, and various old rose hybrids such as the noisette and the damask. Tea roses are beautifully formed and have the happy faculty of blooming over and over again all through the growing season. They have, however, two serious faults: they are weak-necked, the blooms tending to droop on the stems, and they won't stand cold winters.

It is strange how old names persist. Tea roses are scarcely grown any more on this continent, except in very warm, mild areas, such as southern California, Florida, and Louisiana. The modern hybrid tea, which was first introduced in 1867, is far superior in every respect to both of its parents, the tea rose and the hybrid perpetual, yet is is still miscalled after the less desirable of its forebears.

The first hybrid tea, La France, was a big, pink, fragrant rose produced by a French nursery, Guillot Fils. Its parentage is a matter of some doubt—early hybridists often kept inexact records, and were not above publishing deliberate misinformation; at that time, remember, hybridists were not protected by plant patents. However, it is generally believed that the female parent was a large, very fragrant, crimson hybrid perpetual rose called Mme. Victor Verdier, and that the male parent was a white, fragrant tea rose called Mme. Bravy. The result of this union, La France, combined the best characteristics of its two parents. From the tea rose father it inherited a fine, urn-shaped flower form and a tendency to bloom repeatedly from early summer till fall. From its hybrid perpetual mother it inherited great resistance to frost, a good upright stance, strong stems, and exquisite fragrance.

Rose gardens have never been the same since.

Before the hybrid tea, hybrid perpetuals had been the mainstay of the rose cut-flower industry. People still ask their florist for a dozen American Beauty roses, a hybrid perpetual. The florist unabashedly fills the order with a red hybrid tea, such as Better Times, and the customer goes away happy. The rose American Beauty, which goes back to 1875, is one of the better hybrid perpetuals and is fairly typical of the breed. A few hybrid perpetuals are still grown, though some are now classified—

mainly for convenience—as hybrid teas. The bulk of hybrid perpetuals, hundreds and hundreds of varieties, have disappeared from commerce. There are several reasons why the hybrid perpetual was unable to compete with its offspring, the hybrid tea. Hybrid perpetuals tend to make a tremendous burst of bloom at their first flowering in early summer. A good many, but by no means all, come into bloom again early in the fall. Only a handful bloom repeatedly after the fashion of hybrid teas. Obviously, the florist industry would regard the everblooming habit of the hybrid tea as having great economic importance. As for the average gardener, it goes without saying that, offered a choice between a rose that blooms twice a year and one that blooms all summer and fall, he would automatically pick the latter.

Other advantages of the hybrid tea recommended them to rose lovers. Most hybrid perpetuals have a great many petals, from fifty to one hundred, which makes for rather fat blooms, often globular in form. A rose of twenty-five to fifty petals is likely to be much more graceful in form. Many hybrid teas are moderate in their petalage, and while I doubt that many gardeners take the time to count the petals on their roses, they show a great liking for long, slim buds and delicately urn-shaped blooms.

For about thirty years after the first hybrid teas were introduced, their colors were the same as were common in hybrid perpetuals: that is to say, white, pink, and various shades of red. But in 1900 a French hybridist named Joseph Pernet-Ducher brought out a rose so different that for a long time it was given its own classification: pernetiana.

The prototype of the pernetianas was Soleil d'Or

(Golden Sun), a rose that looked and behaved much like a hybrid tea but was a brilliant yellow, lightly shaded with red.

Soleil d'Or resulted from crossing a large, violet-red hybrid perpetual with a wild species, *Rosa foetida,* commonly called the Austrian Briar rose, which has a rather nasty, sickly sweet odor but blossoms of a brilliant gold color. It was the gene for yellow that had been inherited in Soleil d'Or that set it apart from all other garden roses of its time, causing a positive furor among rose growers. Hybridists began growing the new pernetianas and crossing them with hybrid teas. Pernet-Ducher himself continued developing his strain of yellow roses, and in 1920 he produced Souvenir de Claudius Pernet, a very large and exquisitely lovely yellow rose. This particular rose has produced a whole series of distinguished descendants. If you buy a yellow rose today, the chances are very high that somewhere in its pedigree you will find Souvenir de Claudius Pernet.

Pernetiana as a separate classification was soon dropped when the strain became diluted through repeated crossbreeding with hybrid teas. However, Pernet-Ducher's bright idea of using *Rosa foetida* in his breeding program has left us an unwelcome legacy; for along with the gene for yellow, *Rosa foetida* passed on its serious weakness for certain fungus disorders, particularly black spot. The Austrian Briar is notoriously susceptible to black spot, to which the early hybrid teas and the older hybrid perpetuals had been relatively indifferent. There was a period in the twenties and thirties when it seemed that most of the then new roses carried this weakness, regardless of their color, for many pink and red roses had pernetiana blood. Many writers of that period bewailed the weakness to black spot that they observed in the newer roses, and I suspect that this was the source of a widely accepted belief, still prevalent among many gardeners, that the old roses of our grandmothers' days were superior to modern roses.

Ideas, like names, die hard, but there is no longer any foundation for that idea. After all, the rose industry is vitally concerned with such problems as hardiness and disease resistance. Once the weakness of the pernetiana strain was discovered, hybridists bent themselves to the task of breeding black spot resistance back into roses, and in this they have been notably successful.

The part of Tennessee in which I used to live has a most persistent and vigorous strain of black spot, almost impossible to prevent except by the most careful attention to garden sanitation and regular spraying. I had a number of the older types of roses, the sorts to which our grandparents were partial. I have grown many of the roses of the twenties and thirties, and I have grown most of the really significant newer varieties. There is no question whatever in my mind as to the superiority of the new roses over anything previously produced. Particularly since World War II, black spot resistance has been increased to a point where the disease, while still a nuisance, is no longer a menace. The new roses will take it, to be sure, if they are exposed to it, but they seldom die of it if reasonable control measures are employed.

But we still have Pernet-Ducher's gift of the yellow gene, which has resulted in some of the most exquisite colors and color combinations ever seen in roses. Not only such splendid yellow roses as Eclipse, Mrs. Pierre S. Du Pont, Golden Scepter, King's Ransom, and Golden Masterpiece trace back to the pernetiana line, but also bicolored roses, such as Suspense and Forty-Niner, in which the backs of the petals are yellow while the fronts are red; and a whole, wonderful gamut of orange and vermilion roses, such as Tanya, Montezuma, Orange Flame, and Tropicana, not to mention hundreds of varieties in which yellow, gold, and bronze tones are exquisitely blended with white, pink, or red.

Modern hybrid teas really merit the German name *Edelrose.* They stand tall and proud. There are great crimson beauties like Mister Lincoln, Big Red, and Oklahoma, which often open to a diameter of six or seven inches. Mister Lincoln reached a height of six feet in my garden, and it is perhaps the most highly perfumed hybrid tea ever produced. Garden Party, a white rose delicately edged with pale pink, produces enormous blooms in constant profusion on a large, stately bush. Pink Peace, a deep rose-pink bloom of almost perfect form, is nearly as fragrant as Mister Lincoln, grows quite as tall, and seems to shrug off black spot, mildew, and the other diseases to which roses are prone. And then, of course, there is Peace, one of the greatest roses ever produced, which has every desirable quality except fragrance, and a whole progeny of descendants and mutants of Peace that retain their ancestor's great vigor and productivity.

Hybrid teas typically carry one flower per stem. The blooms themselves are finely formed, lovely in all stages, from the tight bud to the fully open flower. They tend to make tall, well-branched bushes and produce many flowering canes. A few are highly fragrant; most have some degree of fragrance. All but a few have a prolonged blooming season—interrupted by short resting periods—that begins with early summer and extends through the fall; in mild-climate areas, such as southern California and central Florida, hybrid teas bloom almost year round. While the foliage of the older hybrid teas is unremarkable, many of the new varieties have leaves of a deep, glossy green reminiscent of holly. With few exceptions, hybrid teas are quite hardy; only in northern regions or places of very high altitude is much winter protection necessary (see page 141).

This, then, is the modern hybrid tea rose, the backbone and mainstay of rose growing today.

Floribundas and Grandifloras

The hybrid tea is prized primarily for its magnificent individual blooms. But as any gardener knows, gardens need a source of massed color, and it is to provide massed color that floribunda roses are most useful.

Modern floribundas are something quite new in the rose world, most of the significant ones having been produced since 1940, largely through the hybridizing efforts of Wilhelm Kordes of Germany and Eugene S. Boerner of the United States; in fact, the latter, until his death in 1966, was affectionately known in the rose trade as "Mr. Floribunda."

Floribundas were developed from an earlier type of rose, the polyantha. Polyanthas are rather compact, low plants that bear hundreds and hundreds of small, pompon blooms in large clusters, much as rambler roses do. Perhaps the best known polyantha in this country is The Fairy, which is sometimes—but to my thinking wrongly—classified as a shrub rose. Not many polyanthas are still on the market, though at one time they were widely sold. Their low stature, combined with their tendency to cover themselves with clusters of flowers, made them highly useful where a mass of color was of more importance than the quality of the individual blooms. The better polyanthas were nearly all the product of a Danish rose breeder, Svend Poulsen, and principally consisted of crosses between two species of roses: *Rosa multiflora*, a very, very hardy Asiatic rose that blooms once a year in vast clusters of small flowers, and *Rosa chinensis*, another Asiatic import, that bears an almost continuous crop of small, red blooms, usually in clusters.

The only serious fault of polyantha roses—"Poulsen roses," they were often called—was that the individual blooms had little in the way of form. They tended to have few petals and to be shaped rather more like carnations than roses. Their advantages were numerous: they were as tough as weeds, generally indifferent to frost and disease, came in a number of pleasant colors—white, pink, red, and various tones of yellow or orange—and made a gratifying display with relatively little attention.

It was to the improvement of the *shape* of the individual blooms of polyantha roses that various plant breeders turned their attention. By crossing polyanthas with hybrid teas, a new and most interesting type of rose was produced. For a long time these new roses were called hybrid polyanthas, but eventually someone thought of the name "floribunda," and it stuck.

Most of the early floribundas retained the low stature of their polyantha ancestors while inheriting something of the blossom form of the hybrid tea. Florists immediately snapped them up as a source of small roses for corsages, and this fact no doubt gave a considerable impetus to further experiments in their breeding. Gardeners also fell in love with them immediately, because they gave fully as much color as polyanthas but were much prettier. Moreover, floribundas proved to have nearly as much resistance to disease and frost as the older polyanthas.

Floribundas typically carried their bloom in clusters or trusses, but the clusters contained fewer individual blooms than those of polyanthas, a fortunate trait that made floribundas suitable for use in arrangements.

As crossbreeding went on, with more and more hybrid tea blood influencing the floribunda strain, varieties were produced that grew quite tall; there began to appear a few whose blooms were typically carried either singly or in clusters of two or three, and the blooms themselves were nearly as large as those of hybrid teas. What to call them? The English burdened themselves with the designation "large-flowered hybrid polyanthas." The French and Germans dubbed them "floribundas," regardless of their difference from the typical floribunda. A number of them, I am reasonably sure, were quietly introduced as hybrid teas. Finally, the term "grandiflora" was attached to them, probably in desperation. Many countries still refuse to recognize "grandiflora" as a legitimate name, largely on the ground that it seems to imply that the individual blooms are unusually large, whereas most grandifloras have somewhat smaller blooms than the larger hybrid teas. The name, however, is current and quite well established in the United States, and since this country has long since taken the lead in the breeding of both floribundas and grandifloras, perhaps we have a moral right to call them what we choose.

What largely distinguishes a grandiflora from a hybrid tea is that most grandifloras bloom more profusely than most hybrid teas. Ultimately, I expect, when the novelty wears off, the same thing will happen to grandifloras that happened to hybrid perpetuals: they will be lumped with the hybrid teas. Personally, I think this is where they belong.

For a long time one particularly valuable characteristic of hybrid teas—fragrance—was almost wholly lacking in floribundas. There were a few that had a slight fragrance, usually of the tea sort, but by comparison with the hybrid teas they were virtually odorless. Shortly before his death, Gene Boerner broke this barrier, as he had broken many others before. His rose, Apricot Nectar, is not only one of the handsomest floribundas yet produced, but it also has a powerful and unmistakable damask rose fragrance.

Floribundas now come in every color and blend of colors found in hybrid teas. There are pure whites, creams, yellows, pinks, lavenders, and reds of every hue. There are clear oranges; delicate blends of pink, gold, and white; and strongly bicolored varieties—the amount of variation is almost endless. And while the typical height of floribundas is from two to three feet, some stand as tall as five feet; others, sometimes known as dwarf floribundas, reach a height of only a foot.

Many of my friends in the rose-growing business disagree vigorously with me in this matter, but it is my opinion that in not too many decades—possibly within my lifetime and surely before the century is over—the present distinction between floribundas and hybrid teas will be obliterated. Not only do floribundas carry a lot of hybrid tea blood, but many of the new hybrid teas have a generous amount of floribunda blood in their ancestry. Plant breeders, seeking to increase the hardiness of hybrid teas and improve their resistance to black spot, are turning to the floribunda and breeding it in hybrid teas. Often nowadays, when a new rose is introduced on the market, it is a tossup whether it will be designated a floribunda, a hybrid tea, or a grandiflora; had you overheard some of the arguments that I have listened to among nurserymen, you would appreciate my point.

Personally, I shan't care what they call them, so long as the present trend in rose breeding continues. Never before in the more than four thousand year history of the rose as a cultivated garden flower have such magnificent roses been produced as in the last thirty years.

Climbers

I really wish I could avoid having to discuss climbers, for of all the major types of roses, they seem to be the hardest to pin down. Like French verbs, there are more exceptions than rules. However, no rose book would be complete without adequate discussion of climbing roses, so I shall have to do my best and hope that it will not leave you confused.

In the first place, no rose is really a climber—at least, not in the sense that ivy and clematis are climbers. Climbers are merely roses that have excessively long canes. Left to their own devices, and allowed to grow without support, climbers will either spraddle all over the ground or develop into large, fountain-shaped bushes similar to forsythia. The French call climbing roses *roses sarmenteux*, which might be translated as "runner roses," in reference to the extremely long canes they develop.

Attempts to classify climbing roses have been both numerous and unsatisfying. Some classifications are based primarily upon the growth habits of the plants. There are some types that put out a number of relatively thin, flexible canes every year, constantly renewing themselves from the base. These plants typically bloom very heavily in early summer, bearing great masses of rather small flowers in clusters or trusses. The open flowers tend to be rather flat and have a great many tiny petals. Such roses are commonly called "ramblers." Some authorities prefer to make a separate category of ramblers and to reserve the term "climber" for a type that makes a small number of very heavy, stiff basal canes from which quantities of side canes, or "laterals," develop. Such bushes usually bear rather large blooms, often carried singly on individual stems, and may either bear on and off all season or have one large flowering in the early summer and a second flowering in the fall. Still other authorities lump them all together as climbing roses.

Another attempt at classification—often encountered in rose catalogues—is based upon blooming habits. Thus we find the term "large-flowered climber" used to distinguish those roses that bear conventionally shaped blooms on individual stems, and "cluster-blooming climbers" to include ramblers and some climbing types of polyantha and floribunda roses. I don't think much of that classification either.

Still based fundamentally upon blooming habits is another sort of classification, in which roses that bloom only once a year are distinguished both from those that bloom twice a year and from those that bloom more or less continuously throughout the season. I don't know of any term for the once-bloomers—catalogue writers tend to play down this habit. The twice-blooming sorts are called either "repeat-blooming" or "remontant," the latter being a term borrowed from the French, while the term "everblooming" is applied to those that bloom on and off all season.

A great many climbing roses develop as sports, botanical mutations of various sorts of garden roses. Thus a hybrid tea growing in somebody's garden may suddenly begin to grow enormously long canes. Sometimes when this occurs the plant virtually gives up blooming. I had this happen once with a plant of Dixie Belle that suddenly grew to a height of over seven feet. But as it then quit blooming for all practical purposes, I finally discarded it, not without some disappointment, as I had hoped that I might have a valuable, patentable Climbing Dixie Belle which would have made me moderately rich. Others have been luckier. Time after time ordinary, relatively low-growing rose bushes have spontaneously turned into spectacular climbers. And this fact has led to the classifications "climbing hybrid tea," "climbing floribunda," and "climbing miniature," and such catalogue names as Cl. Crimson Glory, Cl. Peace, Cl. Goldilocks, and Cl. Pinocchio. Most of the climbing sports of hybrid teas put on one spectacular show and then quit for the summer, while the climbing floribundas tend to be almost everblooming.

I wish this were all it was necessary to say about climbers, but there is one piece of information that I can't very well omit. Some climbers are given a special designation: "pillar rose." This is a rather loose, indeterminate category involving a number of climbers that grow to a moderate height—perhaps six or eight feet—

and make canes stiff enough to stand without support or with a minimum of support. Some of the finest ever-blooming climbers fall into the pillar rose class. Just to make everything thoroughly confusing, pillar roses are often referred to as "semiclimbers."

The classification of roses in general and of climbers in particular makes me think of a German saying: "Why be simple when, with a little more effort, one can be so wonderfully complicated?"

11

A Brief Acquaintance with Some Other Types of Roses

In 1958 the American Rose Society recognized 7,562 varieties and 333 species of roses. Since then, the number has been swollen by several thousand new varieties, and there is no end in sight. As I indicated before, the study of roses is a complex and absorbing topic.

So far, we have been concerned only with the more commonly grown types of roses. There remain a few less well known types with which you should have at least a nodding acquaintance; many of them are beautiful and charming and have their place, along with the newer roses, in domestic landscaping.

Hybrid Perpetuals

These roses have already been briefly described in discussing the origin of hybrid teas. Most of them have disappeared from the market. I have in my possession an 1885 catalogue of the Dingee & Conard Company of West Grove, Pennsylvania, predecessors of the present Conard-Pyle Company, and out of curiosity I made a count of the roses offered in this old catalogue. As nearly as I can determine—it being possible that I might have counted twice some roses that appeared in different lists —the company offered about 212 different hybrid perpetuals, 176 teas, 20 hybrid teas, 17 climbers, 19 moss roses, 7 polyanthas, and 1 cabbage rose, for a grand total of 452 varieties. By contrast, the Fall 1973 Conard-Pyle catalogue offers 57 hybrid teas and grandifloras, which they lump together; 16 floribundas; 6 miniatures; 12 climbers; and 2 shrub roses—in all, 94 varieties.

Still in pursuit of the hybrid perpetual, I consulted the catalogues of two firms that specialize in old roses: The Joseph J. Kern Rose Nursery, Mentor, Ohio, and Will Tillotson's Roses, Watsonville, California. Between them, they offered about one hundred varieties of hybrid perpetuals.

My own experience with hybrid perpetuals has been limited; I have grown Frau Karl Druschki (now usually classified with hybrid teas), Mabel Morrison, Black Prince, Heinrich Munch, and Marchioness of Londonderry. Of these, I came to grow and cherish Heinrich Munch and Mabel Morrison. I consider that both of these roses compare favorably with the best of modern roses, though Heinrich dates from 1911 and Mabel from 1878. What appeals to me particularly about both of them, aside from the fact that they have exquisitely beautiful and delicate flowers, is that they are as tough as sole leather. Insects, disease, and frost seem to have little effect on them. Both get black spot, but it doesn't seem to hinder them particularly. If I were a rose hybridist, I think I'd try back-breeding these roses into modern hybrid teas, just to see what would result.

Most hybrid perpetuals make plants of about the same general stature as hybrid teas and grandifloras, and can be used along with the newer roses. Heinrich Munch, however, makes a whopping great plant; I find it best to grow him as a low climber against a fence or trellis, where he has room to spread out.

You will recall that the everblooming tendency of hybrid teas was largely responsible for their general replacement of hybrid perpetuals. Most of the latter either bloom only once a season or repeat in the fall. There are a few hybrid perpetuals that bloom about as freely as most hybrid teas: I could mention American Beauty, Arillaga, Baroness Rothschild, Baronne Prévost, Everest, Frau Karl Druschki (now usually classified with hybrid teas), Ferdinand Pichard, General Jacqueminot, Georg Arends, Heinrich Munch, Henry Nevard, Mabel Morrison, Mrs. John Laing, and Paul Neyron, and there must be still others.

While I am of the opinon that modern hybrid teas, in general, are a distinct improvement over hybrid perpetuals, I still think there is room in the average rose garden for one or two of these older roses.

Rugosas and Rugosa Hybrids

There are several species of *Rosa rugosa* that occur wild in Asia, particularly China, Japan, and Korea. We need not be concerned with mentioning all of the species; three of them seem to have been widely used, either in their natural form or hybridized with other roses: *Rosa rugosa Thunberg, Rosa rugosa alba,* and *Rosa rugosa rubra.* All rugosas have one characteristic that seems invariably to show up in the hybrids: the leaves are rugose, that is to say, they have a wrinkled appearance caused by the very heavy veining. The foliage is of a good dark color, slightly glossy, and extremely profuse.

The outstanding merit of rugosas, which they seem to pass on to their hybrid offspring, is extreme vigor, hardiness, and resistance to all sorts of pests. I sprayed my rugosas along with other roses, but I suspect it was a waste of time, as they never seemed to have any foliage problems and the bugs left them alone.

Most of the wild species of rugosas have single flowers, varying in color from white to pink to red. Bloom tends to be recurrent all summer, and the flowers are followed by large hips of a bright red color, looking much like small crab apples. While there is a considerable amount of variation in the height of the wild species, most of them seem to make bushes from three to six feet tall, and quite broad in proportion to their height. Several of the wild species are grown, among them *Rosa rugosa magnifica,* which gets about five feet tall and has purplish red blooms; *Rosa rugosa rubra,* which is rather similar; and *Rosa rugosa alba,* which has fragrant white flowers, like large pear blossoms.

As for the hybrid rugosas, no generality will fit them to describe their appearance. The reason for this is not far to seek. I took the trouble to look up the parentage of a number of hybrid rugosas, and found that there is no particular or consistent breeding pattern. I'm sure what has happened is that various plant breeders, admiring the rugosa's hardiness and free-flowering tendencies, have tried crossing it with a number of different roses. Two of the best-known hybrid rugosas are F. J. Grootendorst and Pink Grootendorst, both the products of a competent if immodest Dutchman named Grootendorst. The pink is a mutation of the other one. F. J. Grootendorst resulted from crossing *Rosa rugosa rubra* with a polyantha rose. F. J. Grootendorst bears quantities of small, dark red blooms similar to those of polyanthas—lots of petals and no form. Both Grootendorsts are rather low growing, around three feet. They do have the merit of being very tough and of blooming quite freely, and are rather commonly used for hedges.

Several hybrid rugosas have tea rose blood, particularly Conrad Ferdinand Meyer, a big pink rose that will climb to eight or ten feet if supported, and Blanc Double de Coubert, a double white rose that reaches a height of about six feet and is extremely fragrant.

The hybrid rugosa Ruskin has hybrid perpetual blood, is a brilliant red, and repeatedly produces great clusters of hybrid-perpetual shaped blooms. It is highly fragrant and makes a bush four or five feet tall. Like other hybrid rugosas, it seems to have all the hardiness expected of its rugosa blood.

At least one hybrid rugosa, Dr. Eckner, and possibly

also Sarah Van Fleet, resulted from crossing rugosas with hybrid teas. The former has pink blooms with yellow bases, large, fragrant, and semidouble, making a big bush over five feet tall; the latter, equally fragrant, has big, semidouble pink blooms and may go to eight feet in height.

Finally, there is the hybrid rugosa Max Graf, probably a cross between a rugosa and *Rosa wichuraiana*, a Japanese wild rose with pronouncedly trailing growth habits. Max takes after his Japanese father, and makes a splendid ground cover for banks and other awkward spots, trailing his long canes all over the ground. The flowers, which arrive in one spectacular burst of bloom, are large pink singles with handsome yellow stamens.

I've been saving one hybrid rugosa for last. It goes under the wholly inappropriate name Delicata. As far as the bush goes, it is about the least delicate thing I have ever grown. Once I planted one bush of Delicata, with perhaps four original canes about eighteen inches tall. Four years later it made a solid clump four feet wide, six feet long, and nearly six feet tall. It bloomed continuously for three or four months every summer, producing large, double pink blooms, intensely fragrant, with prominent yellow stamens. God knows what size it might ultimately assume. I did nothing for it except to spray it now and then, an attention it probably didn't need. Once in a while, two or three leaves would show a trace of black spot, but the infection never seemed to spread. I think the plant killed it.

It appears to me that Delicata is a natural choice for foundation planting and for use in hedges. From experience I know that cutting it back only makes it grow more profusely and densely. If you plant Delicata, give it lots of room and then stand back out of the way!

One of these days some smart hybridist is going to go seriously to work on the rugosas. Personally, I think the obvious thing to do would be to cross them with *Rosa chinensis*, to which the hybrid tea, through its tea ancestor, largely owes its everblooming characteristics.

In fact, I may try it myself.

Tea Roses

The principal attraction of the tea rose is the exquisite form of the blooms: long, tapering buds that develop into graceful, urn-shaped flowers. They have a grace that most of the hybrid perpetuals lack, and it was this grace of form that they contributed to the hybrid tea, along with the tendency to bloom repeatedly all season. No doubt another characteristic that made the tea rose popular with our grandparents was the color range, which extended into buff, yellow, and orange tones wholly lacking in hybrid perpetuals. The biggest objection to tea roses, other than the fact that many of them were weak-necked, was that they would not endure heavy winter frosts. There were a few exceptions, such as Safrano, G. Narbonnand, General Schablikine, and Mrs. Dudley Cross, which might endure temperatures as low as zero. However, tea roses usually had to be raised in greenhouses or cold frames, except in areas where freezing weather was virtually unknown. Nearly all tea roses are practically immune to black spot, an excellent point in their favor. Their fragrance is spicy rather than sweet, which some people find most intriguing; personally, I prefer the damask rose scent of good hybrid teas and hybrid perpetuals.

If I lived in southern California, Bermuda, Puerto Rico, southern Louisiana or on the Gulf Coast, I would probably have a go at raising tea roses. Under the right conditions, largely a matter of climate, they make big bushes and bloom enthusiastically.

Gallicas, Damasks, and Bourbons

Rosa gallica is generally conceded to be the earliest known ancestor of modern garden roses. Its own origins are obscure, but it appears to have developed in the Near East, presumably from some still earlier Asiatic rose now lost or unidentifiable. Roses of the gallica type were known and grown as garden flowers in the eastern Mediterranean area at least two thousand years before Christ. Botanists conjecture that the earliest gallicas bore very double red blooms with a pronounced sweet fragrance. Such roses were known and grown by the Greeks, by the Romans, and by the Egyptians. During the Middle Ages the gallica reached France, where one particularly highly scented form of it, the Apothecary's Rose, was grown for the production of rose attar and for making various salves and perfumes, many of which were believed to have medicinal value. The term "gallica" no doubt reflects the exploitation of this rose in France. In any case, once the gallicas became common in France, many varieties were developed either through chance hybridization or selection of promising seedlings, and today most gallicas have French names. Gallica blood can be traced through nearly all of the modern roses.

Gallicas have an upright growth habit with many shoots; the foliage is dull and rough to the touch; the thorns are small and nearly straight. The bushes tend to grow into clumps or thickets unless they are budded on an understock; own-root plants quickly spread from root suckers.

The particular charm of gallicas, to those who admire them, is their tendency to lavender and purple shades; to me, this constitutes a fault—I like reds and pinks unadulterated with blue—but many people feel exactly the opposite. *De gustibus non disputandum est.*

Gallicas bloom only once a year, but, as is the case with most roses that have this blooming habit, they make a lavish display while they are at it. Their size, from three to five feet in height, makes them better suited to use as shrubs or foundation plantings than as bedding roses; and for this purpose, or as hedge roses, they are worth trying. After all, other flowering shrubs like lilac and kerria and mock orange aren't expected to bloom continuously, so why expect it of shrub roses? The toughness and general ease of cultivation that characterize gallicas recommend them highly. If you would like to try a few, here are some reliable varieties: *Rosa gallica officinalis* (the Apothecary's Rose); Alain Blanchard; Camaieux; and Cardinal de Richelieu.

Damask roses are thought to be the progeny of gallicas. In antiquity two very ancient and quite distinct types were grown in the Mediterranean area: *Rosa damascena* and *Rosa damascena bifera*. The Near East origins of both are evident in the name "damask," that is, from Damascus.

Rosa damascena, which blooms only once a year, is thought to be a chance hybrid between *Rosa gallica* and *Rosa phoenicia; Rosa damascena bifera* is believed to be a cross between *Rosa gallica* and *Rosa moschata*, the musk rose.

The repeat-blooming habit of *Rosa damascena bifera*, which produces two vigorous flowerings per year, made it particularly valuable to gardeners and florists of antiquity. The Romans seized on it with delight, and set up a flourishing cut-flower industry in competition with Egyptian florists, who hitherto had had a corner on the Roman market. With characteristic energy and ingenuity (the possibility of profit always worked wonders on the Roman mind) they figured out how to build greenhouses heated with hot-water pipes, and in them, at the very beginning of the Christian era, produced hothouse roses in the dead of winter.

Like the gallicas, the damasks are highly fragrant. One variety, Kazanlik, is the basis of the European perfume industry. The fact that modern damasks are descended from the two main types, *Rosa damascena*, a once-blooming type, and *Rosa damascena bifera*, which repeats its bloom, accounts for the fact that damasks have long been divided into two types, summer damasks and autumn damasks; the former make only one annual show of bloom, while the latter are repeat blooming. Some of the autumn damasks, in fact, bloom almost continuously. There are some differences in the appearance of the canes and in the growth habits of the two types, but I don't think they need concern us here.

Most of the damasks make rather large bushes, not too well suited by reason of their size for use in rose beds. Like the gallicas, I believe they lend themselves better

27

to use as specimen shrubs. The colors of damasks are more pleasing to me than those of gallicas: good whites, pinks, and deep reds. Many have extremely double blooms of good size, which tend to bloom in moderate clusters, rather like floribundas. At least one variety of autumn damask, Rose de Rescht, makes a low compact plant, bears highly perfumed bright red blooms, and is suitable for growing with floribundas or hybrid teas. Another, Rose du Roi, which was one of the early ancestors of the hybrid perpetual, makes large, red semi-double crimson blooms; repeats freely; and would not be out of place among hybrid teas. If you try Rose du Roi, which wouldn't be a bad idea, place it where it has room to grow, for the bush is rather spreading. Like the gallicas, the damasks can get along with little care, but will probably do better if you give them the same consideration you would offer your hybrid teas and floribundas.

Bourbon roses are in some respects more like modern roses than either the gallicas or the damasks. The foliage looks much like that of a hybrid tea or a floribunda, and the general air and appearance of the plant are familiar to growers of modern roses. Bourbons resulted from a chance crossing of damasks with China roses, which occurred early in the nineteenth century on the island of Bourbon (now called Réunion) in the Indian Ocean.

In the ancestry of the Bourbon rose, we have something rather similar to that of the hybrid perpetual and hybrid tea, particularly the latter: tea roses are a type of China rose. Not only is the foliage similar to that of modern roses, but many Bourbons bloom in much the same manner as hybrid teas, producing repeated crops of flowers all summer and fall. Most Bourbons differ markedly from hybrid teas in the shape of the blooms; they tend to have rather globular flowers with many short petals, and the open rose is often "quartered," that is, the petals clump around three or four central points, instead of around a single point. Quartering is regarded as a fault in hybrid teas, though many otherwise fine varieties display it; but to fanciers of old roses, quartering is quaint and charming. I must admit I find this form a pleasing change.

There are a number of good Bourbons that can be grown along with hybrid teas and floribundas. Both La Reine Victoria and Madame Pierre Oger—the first deep pink, the second pale pink—can be used with hybrid teas if they are given a little extra room in which to spread. The blooms are strongly cupped, with many petals, and are highly perfumed. My favorite Bourbon, however, is a modest little plant called Souvenir de la Malmaison, as free-blooming as any modern floribunda. The flowers are very double, rather cupped, and strongly quartered; the fragrance is intense; and the large blooms are light pink, deepening in the centers. I've observed that people never pass by a blooming plant of Malmaison.

One other Bourbon merits attention. Called Gloire des Rosomanes in Europe, it is well known in this country as Ragged Robin. It is used both as an understock for the budding of roses and as a hedge rose. It makes a head-high hedge calling for little care, and carries a lot of bright red blooms.

Hybrid Musks and Other Shrub Roses

The musk rose, *Rosa moschata*—which, you will recall, probably entered into the makeup of the autumn damask rose—has given rise to a number of hybrids. Many of the old rambler roses, which had a tendency to bloom in huge clusters of small blossoms, were of the "noisette" type, derived by crossing *Rosa chinensis* with *Rosa moschata*. They made handsome climbers, but were not very hardy. An English clergyman, the Reverend Mr. J. H. Pemberton, who did a great deal of rose hybridizing, developed more than twenty varieties, most of them cluster flowering, by breeding then existent hybrids of *Rosa moschata* (known as "noisette roses"), with various other roses, notably hybrid teas, hybrid perpetuals, and tea roses. A study of the parentage of most of Pemberton's roses discloses that many of them came from crosses in which the noisette-type climber Trier was either the maternal parent or grandparent. Whatever may have been the Reverend Mr. Pemberton's goal in hybridizing, he succeeded in developing a number of rather tall (four- to six-foot), somewhat informal varieties that bloom freely and repeatedly, usually in clusters of small flowers, and are quite hardy. Colors range from white and buff through various shades of yellow and pink to bright red; some varieties show semidouble or double blooms, but most are of the single type. In the first quarter of this century, when Pemberton was most active, hybrid musks were commonly referred to as "Pemberton roses."

Not all hybridists who have developed hybrid musks

followed the same pattern of breeding. A very satisfactory hybrid musk rose, Bishop Darlington, which I grew for several years, is a cross between one of Pemberton's roses and a rambler; from the latter parent it got some *Rosa wichuraiana* blood and another admixture of noisette blood, presumably thus reinforcing the musk rose characteristics. Bishop Darlington looks almost wholly different from the other musk roses. It bears its blooms singly but in considerable number on a moderate-sized bush. The flowers are almost single, quite large, and go through an interesting color change: the opening buds are cherry red; as the blooms open wider, they turn to a flesh pink tinged with yellow. They are sweetly fragrant and the bush is never wholly without them. It and the hybrid rugosa Delicata, which grew next to it, were the last roses to quit blooming in our garden each fall, and then only when hard frosts occurred.

Although some people grow hybrid musks with other roses in beds, I think they should be treated as specimen shrubs and grown either singly or in groups of two or three. As foundation shrubs they are hard to beat, requiring practically nothing in the way of pruning and trimming. Bishop Darlington shows a mild susceptibility to black spot, but doesn't seem to be bothered greatly by it, and I have seldom seen any indication of insect damage on this rose.

Several hybrid musks are best known as hedge roses; I expect that Robin Hood and Will Scarlett are the two best for this purpose. They will quickly make a dense, handsome hedge. Robin Hood grows to four or five feet tall, while Will Scarlett makes a lower hedge, about waist high. Both bear profuse quantities of bright red blooms.

31

Centifolia roses, commonly known as "cabbage roses," are of ancient origin in Europe and are believed to have developed by chance hybridizing with *Rosa damascena*. I dislike most of them acutely for several reasons: the blooms are as round as a ball, with the petals closely overlapped like the leaves of a cabbage; this I find absurd. They bloom only once a year, and as the foliage is unremarkable and the plants carry their leaves rather high and sparsely on long prickly canes, mainly bare at the base, I think the bush is ugly after the flowering is over. However, they do have their good points: they are undeniably tough, and they smell wonderful.

There is one centifolia that I have grown in the past and would be glad to grow again: Petite de Hollande. The bush grows with astonishing vigor to a height of about four feet, pushing up cane after cane till it makes a small thicket. The canes, being long and rather slim, tend to arch over in fountain shape, which increases under the almost incredible load of small, pink blooms that they bear in clusters of four or five to a stem. The buds are so round they are like little marbles, but they open up wide and rather flat, after the fashion of the blooms of a rambler. When Petite de Hollande is in flower, it is positively spectacular—pretty enough so that I can forgive its rather naked look for the rest of the year. This particular centifolia, I think, is worth growing with other flowering shrubs.

All of which brings me to the moss rose, a mutation of the centifolia. The rose gets its common name from the fact that the sepals and sometimes the upper part of the stem immediately below the flower are covered with a prickly growth resembling moss. This spontaneously appearing phenomenon—centifolia roses with green fuzz

on them—sent seventeenth-century gardeners into rap-
tures, and the moss was soon perpetuated in a number
of hybrids. The original moss roses bloomed only once a
year, but some of their progeny flower repeatedly.

Personally, I dislike them. To me they are grotesque,
although other people find them lovely beyond words.
I mention them principally because they can be grown
without much trouble as shrubs, and if you like them at
all you will probably end by being crazy about them.
Common Moss, Chapeau de Napoléon (Crested Moss),
and Deuil de Paul Fontaine are varieties greatly admired
by moss-rose enthusiasts; the last mentioned is a repeat
bloomer. And there are many other sorts from which
to choose, including some miniature varieties.

We come now to a miscellany of roses that make very
large shrubs, and that are best used as one would use forsythia, weigela, or japonica. To classify them all would
be wearisome, and probably unnecessary for the average
rose lover.

Rosa hugonis, Father Hugo's Rose or Golden Rose of
China, is a Chinese wild rose that has single yellow
blooms. It makes a tall bush of delicate weeping canes
and fernlike leaves, bearing one heavy crop of blooms
early in the season. Flowers appear all up and down the
stems, after the fashion of forsythia blooms. The bushes
usually stand about six feet tall, but may go higher.
They prefer rather poor soil, and do best if not fertilized.

Hon. Lady Lindsay is a cross between a climber and
a hybrid tea. The result is a tall, bushy shrub bearing
large, fragrant pink blooms of hybrid tea form. The
rose is hardy, has good resistance to pests, and blooms
repeatedly.

33

Rosa moyesii, another Chinese species, is unique in that the hips or fruits that follow the bloom are very large, bright red, and shaped like little bottles. Several hybrids have been developed that make valuable shrubs, particularly Nevada, which has very large, single white blooms with prominent gold stamens, and Geranium, which has bright red single blooms about two inches in diameter. Like most roses from China, the *moyesii* hybrids are hardy and resistant, requiring little care. Nevada makes a bush about six feet tall; Geranium tends to be shorter.

Mabelle Stearns, like Hon. Lady Lindsay, is the result of crossing a climber with a hybrid tea. From its climber mother it gets a lot of the blood and hardiness of *Rosa setigera,* a wild rose native to this country. The resulting hybrid makes a large, tough bush and produces quantities of small, pink, fragrant blooms resembling those of a floribunda. The bush is only two or three feet tall, but spreads to as much as six feet in diameter.

In discussing polyanthas in the previous chapter, I mentioned a rose called The Fairy, one of the toughest and most floriferous roses I have ever seen. Like Mabelle Stearns, it makes a low, wide, sprawling bush, covered most of the season with an astonishing load of flowers: small, pink, very double blooms borne in large clusters. If it is grown on its own roots, it will sucker freely from the base and soon turn into a very large clump. My experience is that it needs spraying against black spot, which disfigures its appearance but doesn't seem to hurt its exuberant high spirits. It also seems to bloom and thrive better for being sheared occasionally, the best time being immediately after one flowering has been finished. The Fairy makes a good companion rose to Mabelle Stearns.

The great German hybridst Wilhelm Kordes gave much attention to the breeding of shrub roses and produced some beauties. Among his best are Elmshorn (clear red double blooms in clusters); Sparrieshoop (large, semisingle pink blooms in clusters); Nymphenburg (cupped, salmon-orange blooms in clusters); and Frülingsmorgen (very large, bright yellow single blooms edged with pink). All of these make tough, highly disease-resistant shrubs four to six feet tall. Another Kordes rose, which I regard as one of his triumphs, is Kassel; it can either be used as a moderate climber or as a self-supporting shrub. It makes an immense bush, six or eight feet tall and fully as broad, with handsome dark green, glossy leaves. The flowers, which are borne in constant succession, seemingly without rest, are like perfect little hybrid tea roses of a startling burnt-orange color. All of the Kordes roses mentioned here are everblooming in the true sense of the term.

Miniatures

Not all of the curiosities of rosedom are pleasing. Nothing, to my eye, could be less attractive, for example, than the so-called Green Rose, *Rosa chinensis viridens*, unaccountably grown and cherished by some rose gardeners. Its blooms are misshapen and its petals are of a nasty leaf-green color. However, though miniature roses are also a definite curiosity, they are charming and delightful in their own small way.

If you want to know what miniature roses look like,

examine an ordinary floribunda or hybrid-tea bush through the wrong end of a pair of binoculars. Stems, thorns, leaves, and flowers are very like those of their larger relatives—merely greatly reduced in scale. Few varieties have flowers as large as an inch in diameter; most are about as big around as a nickel when fully open. A mature bush may stand from eight inches to a foot tall, and some are much shorter. There are also a few miniatures designated as "climbing" that, with luck, may reach a height of three or four feet. Like polyanthas and floribundas, to which they are closely related, miniatures tend to bloom in clusters and to continue blooming over a very long season.

Since they come in a good selection of colors—red, pink, yellow, white, and even lavender—they lend themselves to tasteful combinations in small beds of their own; to patio or walk edging; to use in rock gardens along with small annuals and perennials; and to growing in containers. Flower arrangers find them exciting material: they make delightful corsages, and I have seen charming arrangements in which an eggcup served as the vase. By and large, miniatures do best outdoors, but some people are quite successful at raising them indoors.

The origins of the miniature rose are somewhat obscure. Much of the information I have been able to secure about them was kindly supplied by the Conard-Pyle Company, which is largely responsible for the introduction and popularization of these roses, but a lot remains either legend or pure conjecture.

It is an established fact that, around 1810, somebody brought a miniature rose variety to England, presumably from China or Japan. It would appear to have been a form of *Rosa chinensis minima*, a dwarf strain of *Rosa chinensis,* the species that has contributed so much to the breeding of larger garden roses. The first type introduced into England was originally called *Rosa pusilla,* but later, in 1815, it was renamed Miss Lawrence's Rose in honor of Miss Mary Lawrence, a well-known artist who specialized in flower painting. From this name came the designation "Lawrenceana," which was applied to the few new varieties that were shortly produced from the original parent stock.

About a quarter century after the miniatures were introduced in England and Europe, they disappeared and no one seems to have the faintest idea why. In any case, a century went by before they were rediscovered. There is even some doubt about how this took place. The commonly accepted story is that one Major Roulet, while engaged in a walking tour, found six-inch rose plants with red blossoms growing in window boxes in a Swiss Alpine village and took some plants to the Geneva nurseryman, Henri Correvon, who set about propagating them. Correvon named the variety Rouletti, after its discoverer, and introduced it about 1930.

By 1933, an engaging Dutchman, John de Vink of Boskoop, Netherlands, who had a tiny nursery business, was busily crossing plants of Rouletti with just about every rose he had handy, often using mixed pollens from several varieties. A most unscientific breeding program, but one that worked spectacularly well. While the parentage is problematical, de Vink was of the opinion that it was pollen from the orange-red polyantha Gloria Mundi that did the trick and resulted in a brand-new red miniature with a white center. The late Robert Pyle of the Conard-Pyle Company was enchanted with it and introduced it in 1936 under the name Tom Thumb.

Since then miniature roses have had a considerable vogue.

While de Vink can be rightly credited with developing about a score of new miniatures, most of which were introduced by Conard-Pyle, other plant breeders have gotten into the act. Another Hollander, G. de Ruiter, developed and had introduced a series of very dwarf roses named for the Seven Dwarfs. Although officially classed as polyanthas, they are usually regarded as rather large miniatures.

During World War II, when most of his breeding of large garden roses had to be curtailed, the Spanish hybridist Pedro Dot turned his attention to miniatures and developed a number of new varieties.

The House of Meilland, famous for Peace, along with countless other great roses, have lately busied themselves with breeding miniatures and have contributed some real beauties.

Much is owed to Ralph Moore of Sequoia Nursery, Visalia, California. Mr. Moore has become a specialist in miniatures, having bred and introduced over sixty varieties, several of which are tiny climbers.

Miniatures tend to fall into two types, according to the form of the blooms. The majority of them have flowers that open flat, and have a very large number of quite small petals. The general effect is like that of the flowers of ramblers, or of some of the older polyanthas, such as The Fairy or Mother's Day. A number of the varieties of this type also show sharply pointed rather than rounded tips to the petals. The other type has fewer petals—perhaps thirty to sixty—has rounded petal tips, and produces blooms with the characteristic urn shape of the hybrid tea. On the whole, I find the latter type more charming and satisfying, though I think they make rather less of a color splash than the first sort, not bearing in such large clusters.

My own favorites are Starina, an orange-red with an exquisite urn shape; Pixie Rose, another urn-shaped variety in a deep rose pink with a fine fragrance; Shooting Star, a yellow-and-red blend with sharply pointed petals; and Red Imp, much like a greatly reduced Crimson Glory.

My experience with miniatures is limited. I tried growing them in the front of beds containing larger roses, with little success, though this use is frequently recommended. The big roses—floribundas and hybrid teas—visually overpowered the miniatures and their effect was lost. I have tried them as house plants; they did well until winter, when the drying effect of central heating upset them. They *can* be grown in the house, but special conditions are necessary. They do well in a window greenhouse, where the atmosphere is suitably humid and the plants get plenty of light. Lacking a greenhouse—if you must grow them indoors—put fine gravel in a shallow pan; keep water around the gravel; set the pots of miniatures on the gravel; and keep them either in a sunny window or under fluorescent light.

Like bonsai trees, miniature roses belong outdoors. Despite their small size, they are tough and reliably winter hardy at least as far north as New York City. They are natural subjects for growing in window boxes and patio plant containers, for which their small size and exuberant blooming habits recommend them. They do well, I am told, in rock gardens along with very low-growing flowers like Ageratum, Portulaca, Basket of Gold, Sweet Alyssum, Candytuft, and Moss Pinks.

Best of all, I think, is to give miniature roses a little bed of their own. Be sure to install permanent bed edging, so that the lawn grass can't encroach on the roses: they are too tiny to stand up to much competition for growing space. You can plant them from nine inches to a foot apart, reserving the wider spacing for the taller varieties. You might even erect a little trellis at the back of the bed for a few climbing miniatures, varieties like Climbing Jackie, Little Showoff, or Hi-Ho, set two feet apart. In designing the bed, follow the general principles on the use of roses set forth in Chapter VII. Prepare the soil carefully; keep the plants well mulched, watered, fertilized, and sprayed; and enjoy the particular charm that miniatures exert on most people who grow them.

Appendix D (page 224) describes a number of miniatures.

I I I

Choice Hybrid Teas and Grandifloras

I OUGHT to know better. Anyone who has had any experience of growing roses already has a number of favorite varieties and will want my advice only insofar as it concurs with his own opinions. Yet I feel impelled to suggest a list of my favorites, hybrid teas and grandifloras, which for one reason or another seem to me to be of special merit. The worst of it is that no matter which roses I select, I am bound to omit some that other gardeners would regard as indispensable.

Actually, I suppose this is one of the particular pleasures of rose growing: there are so many lovely roses available that there is plenty of room for argument over their relative merits. Put a dozen rose enthusiasts together, and they will produce a dozen different lists of favorites, having only a few varieties in common.

So I shall proceed to lay myself open to argument and describe those varieties that I find particularly satisfying. In making up the list, I have tried to keep certain qualities in mind. Hardiness—that quality in a plant that enables it to withstand hot, dry summers and severe winters and still come back, year after year—is perhaps the trait that I most admire. Freedom of bloom is high on my list; I want lots of flowers over a long season. I like size—tall, well-bushed plants whose blooms look me in the eye—though I don't insist on it: some of my favorites are of moderate size, both in the plant and in the flower. I want good color: clean, unadulterated colors, not muddied tints. And, if possible, I want fragrance, preferably a good, solid, damask scent.

Not all of the roses I have selected have all of these qualities, but they have most of them. All are varieties that I have known intimately.

In common with most people, when I think of roses the first image that comes to my mind is that of a red rose. I'm sure the red varieties are the favorites of most people who grow roses, and justly so. My list, I'm afraid, is somewhat unbalanced on the side of red roses—but there is such a wealth of varieties from which to choose. There are also a disproportionate number of pink varieties included. No doubt there is a reason for this. Plant breeders seeking to improve roses have only the genes of wild roses from which to produce new and striking varieties—for all cultivated roses go back ultimately to wild species. You will find that pink and red are the two commonest colors among wild rose species; whites and yellows are comparatively rare.

I was discussing this question one day with Gene Boerner, commenting on how rare really good yellows and whites are in comparison to the wealth of excellent reds and pinks, and ventured the suggestion that in developing red and pink varieties we were going *with* rather than *against* the genes. He pondered my remark at some length and finally said that he had never thought of the problem in just that way before, but that he suspected I was quite right.

If you started out to breed dogs from wolves, coyotes, and jackals, think how much simpler it would certainly be to produce wooly brown ones than short-coated white ones.

And now, without further preamble or apology, here is my list of favorite hybrid teas and grandifloras.

Reds

MISTER LINCOLN. Put all of the good qualities you can think of into one rose—a tall, vigorous bush with fine, glossy foliage; six- or seven-inch blooms, exquisitely formed, of a pure, vibrant crimson; long, strong stems; and a full, insistent damask fragrance—and you have Mister Lincoln. I don't always agree with the All-America Rose Selections; sometimes it seems to me that indifferent roses are selected simply because *something* has to be selected every year, but in the case of this variety, I think the award was richly deserved. If I could grow only one crimson rose, it would be this one.

AMERICANA. I have a weakness for this rose, to my mind one of Gene Boerner's finest achievements. It does not have the imposing stature of Mister Lincoln, making a bush only three to four feet tall, nor is it as richly fragrant. It does have everything one could ask in terms of fine foliage, vigor, and generosity of bloom, and the individual blooms are almost, though not quite, as large as those of Mister Lincoln, and quite as beautifully formed. Its special quality is a peculiar luminosity of the color, a bright red. One would almost think that the flowers were lighted from within: a unique trait that I am at a loss either to describe or explain.

SCARLET KNIGHT. This tall, vigorous grandiflora, which was an All-America winner in 1968, is distinguished for its profusion of deep scarlet blooms and its handsome foliage. The buds, which have a refined, classic form, start off a deep crimson and open to a startling scarlet, rather cupped flower four or more inches in diameter. As the blooms open, the petals tend to curl inward, hiding the center, so that the open bloom always presents a tidy appearance. I like this rose especially for its vigor and generosity, and I think you will, too.

OKLAHOMA. This rose is such a dark red that it is very nearly black, and it is almost as fragrant as Mister Lincoln. It excited me when I was sent some test plants a year prior to its introduction, and it proved fascinating to visitors to the Municipal Rose Garden, who always lingered over it. It makes a tall, well-proportioned bush with handsome foliage, blooms freely, and shows plenty of vigor. Its huge, beautifully formed blooms are delightful in arrangements, particularly when their remarkable depth of color is set off with white or clear yellow roses.

CRIMSON GLORY. For many years this deep crimson rose was the standard of excellence by which other red roses were judged. To me, the fact that it has now been surpassed by other, similar reds in no way lowers my esteem for it.

I once asked Gene Boerner which of the roses of other hybridists he wished he had produced himself. Without hesitation, he named Crimson Glory, hybridized by his old friend, the German plant breeder Wilhelm Kordes. I had expected Gene to name Peace, frequently acclaimed as the greatest rose of all time.

Crimson Glory has a magnificent depth of color, uniform on both sides of the petals. It is fully as fragrant as Mister Lincoln, the blooms are beautifully formed, from tight bud to fully open flower, and it is one of the most generous of hybrid teas. Its only real fault is that the bush, which is of medium height, tends to be rather lax and sprawling, thereby encroaching upon its neighbors in the bed. A small fault in the face of so many signal virtues.

MIRANDY. This deep crimson rose, which, like Crimson Glory, is now without patent protection, has much to praise and little to fault. It makes a tall, strong bush of good, upright form and bears generous quantities of very large, heavily perfumed blossoms on long stems. The form of the flowers, particularly in open bloom, is a little more cupped than is now fashionable—but fashions in roses change just as they do in clothing, and with quite as little logic. Personally, I regard Mirandy as a wholly satisfying rose: lovely and reliable.

CHARLOTTE ARMSTRONG. One of the grand old ladies of rosedom, whose blood has gone into some of our most exquisite new roses. I find it hard to classify the color of this rose. Officially it is listed as a light red, but I suppose it might with equal logic be called a very dark pink. Whatever color you call it, it is a lovely rose. Few hybrid teas bloom with as much abandon; in respect to bloom, it almost rivals the floribundas. The individual blooms are exquisitely formed, particularly when in the half-open stage, and if the bush is partially disbudded, very large blooms will be produced. This rose grows into a big, upstanding bush with fine, glossy foliage that shows both hardiness and vigor. Add that the blooms are strongly scented, and I don't see what more you can ask of a rose.

Pinks

PINK PEACE. I find it as easy and natural to select this as my favorite pink rose as it was to select Mister Lincoln among a host of fine red roses. This is one of the most vigorous hybrid teas I have ever encountered, not only in the plant, which is very tall and well branched and produces quantities of strong basal canes, but also in its blooming habits. It bears many blooms at a time, and is seldom out of flower. The color is hard to describe: a deep dusty pink with no hint of lavender, soft yet vibrant. I find it always stands out among other pink roses, partly because of the immense size and really magnificent form of the blooms. Few roses have as much substance to them: the individual petals are huge and quite opaque. A hard-driving rain that will shatter other roses will have little or no effect on the fine, sculptured blooms of Pink Peace. And I know of no rose, not even Mister Lincoln or Crimson Glory, possessing a more potent damask fragrance.

It is always hard to make such choices, but if I had to choose only one rose variety to grow, I think it would be Pink Peace.

MISS ALL-AMERICAN BEAUTY. Occasionally someone

hybridizes a rose that seems to embody wholly feminine characteristics. This is such a rose. The color is a deep, full pink, utterly clear and seductive, uniform on both sides of the petals. The blooms are of exhibition form, with high centers and closely packed petals of great substance. The bush is on the tall side, with handsome, glossy leaves. I can't find anything to fault in this one. The fact that it has a pleasant, light fragrance comes as an added bonus.

First Prize. A posthumous introduction hybridized by the late Gene Boerner, this is about as fine an exhibition rose as I have ever seen. The fronts of the petals are of a light pink, with the edges stained a darker cerise tinge, which is the color of the reverse of the petals. The lightly fragrant buds are unusually large, and open into classically shaped blooms five or six inches in diameter. The plant itself is tall and upright, with highly decorative dark leaves. No wonder First Prize has been taking top honors at rose shows ever since its introduction in 1970.

Royal Highness. An almost ideal exhibition form and a clear, pale pink coloration, similar to that of apple blossoms, distinguish this variety. It is, moreover, highly fragrant. These qualities no doubt prompted its selection as an All-America winner in 1962, and have accounted for its continuing popularity.

My observation on this rose is that it is at its best in cool climate areas. When I grew it in Tennessee, it appeared to suffer more from intense summer heat than many of my other roses, but was really magnificent early in the season and in the fall. During the hot months it tended to sulk. Moreover, thrips sought it out as a special delicacy. Even in the face of these difficulties, however, it was well worth the trouble to grow it. For northern gardeners, or those who live in moist, maritime climates, I would recommend it without reservation.

Columbus Queen. This is a well-named rose: it *does* have the look of royalty. The fronts of the petals are of a medium orchid pink, contrasting strongly with the backs, which are much deeper in tone. The blooms are large and of very nearly perfect exhibition form. The fragrance is only slight, but the rose's distinctive coloration and fine form compensate for this defect. Although the rose has a great delicacy of appearance, it is vigorous and blooms most freely on a large, well-formed bush. I would recommend this rose without reservation: it seems to do beautifully everywhere.

Coral

Whereas prior to the 1960s there were very few coral-pink or coral-orange hybrid teas, now there are quantities of them, all more alike than different. In addition to their unusual coloration, nearly all flower freely, produce unusually large blooms, and make tremendous bushes of great vigor. A few are also highly fragrant.

I find it hard to make a selection of one or two from among all of these handsome new roses. These two, however, have particularly delighted me.

Camelot. This rose, which is officially classed as a grandiflora, was selected for the All-America Rose award in 1965. The color is more on the side of pink than of orange, and varies a little according to the season and temperature; orange tones become more evident in the fall, when the weather turns a bit crisp. The blooms are large, slightly cupped, and quite fragrant. In common with other grandifloras, Camelot is very generous in its flowering. The bushes go to a height of about five feet, and show much resistance to frost damage.

HAWAII. This huge, coral-orange rose was the first of a whole series of roses of its type to be introduced by the Jackson & Perkins rose nursery; nearly all of them were the work of Gene Boerner. The blooms are seldom less than six inches in diameter when fully open, and are produced in great profusion on extremely large, tall, vigorous bushes. Not all of the coral hybrid teas are fragrant, but this one has an exceptionally satisfying perfume. Both Hawaii and Camelot belong in the back row of the bed, with plenty of elbow room.

White

Every rose bed needs a few white roses because nothing else does quite as much to show off the colors of other roses. Unfortunately, really outstanding white roses are scarce. Even the best of them fall far short of pinks and reds in reliability of bloom.

BLANCHE MALLERIN. To my mind, this is the most generally satisfactory white rose I have grown or observed. Many rosarians would take issue with me on this matter, I am sure, and name some other white rose in its place. However, I like this one. If it has a fault, it is that the petals are a little thinner than they should be, making them more liable to rain damage than some newer varieties. However, the rose makes up for this slight defect by having a wealth of desirable qualities. The blooms are of clear, clean white with no hint of ivory or green, commonly encountered in other white varieties. The form of the blooms is remarkable: the classic urn shape at its best. The plant is tall, strong, and upright and grows with much vigor, whereas many other white roses make small bushes and seem to begrudge every inch of growth. Few white roses are fragrant, but this one is. Finally, it has been on the market since 1941 and its patent has long since expired; consequently, it can be purchased for a very moderate price.

GARDEN PARTY. Officially, this is not a white rose. Its huge blooms show a faint tinge of pale shell pink around the petal edges, particularly in cool weather. But the effect of Garden Party in a bed is that of a white rose, adding snap to all the colors around it. In really hot weather, which tends to daunt pure white roses, Garden Party unconcernedly produces a wealth of huge blooms showing almost no coloration. I choose, therefore, to classify it among the whites, though it is technically a blend.

Few roses can approach Garden Party in terms of generosity of bloom and plant vigor. I'm sure its ancestry accounts for these splendid qualities: it is a cross between Charlotte Armstrong and Peace, and tends to inherit some of the best qualities of both parents. It is one of those roses that looks utterly feminine and delicate but is as tough as a weed. It lacks only one thing: fragrance. So far I haven't missed it.

Yellows

ECLIPSE. This is a great and significant rose, whose blood has gone into a long line of distinguished newer varieties. It goes back to a tiny seedling that showed up in Jackson & Perkins's greenhouse in 1932, one of a large number hybridized there by Dr. J. H. Nicolas, an engaging Frenchman who made great contributions to the improvement of roses. The plant, a real runt, put out a single, deep gold bloom on August 31, 1932, a day when most Americans, myself included, were watching a total eclipse of the sun. The seedling was so tiny that Dr. Nicolas was in some doubt as to whether he dared rob it of its two or three bud eyes so that they could be grafted to understock. In any case, the budding was a success, and the rose was finally introduced in 1935. It proceeded to win nearly all of the important rose awards, and still compares very favorably with the best modern yellows. There are newer varieties that have larger blooms—Eclipse is of only moderate size—and varieties that make larger bushes and bloom more profusely. Yet Eclipse retains its universal popularity. I think the real secret of this rose's success is the perfection of its buds, so long, so exquisitely shaped, so utterly refined as to defy description.

GOLDEN GIRL. Officially classed as a grandiflora, this rose does grow much like a grandiflora: tall, vigorous, and very free-blooming. However, a study of its parentage does not disclose any floribunda or polyantha blood; to my mind, the variety should be listed as a hybrid tea. In any case, it is lovely and very satisfactory, closely related to both Eclipse and Peace. I think this is probably the easiest of all yellows to grow; it's the one I always recommend to beginners. Most yellow roses are a bit temperamental, but not Golden Girl, which blooms most freely and rests very seldom. The quality of the blooms is unusually good. While the buds are not quite as refined in appearance as those of Eclipse, the open flowers are much better. When Eclipse is fully open, it loses much of its shape, probably because it doesn't have enough petals. Golden Girl, however, like Peace, produces a bloom of considerable substance that holds its shape well until it begins to wilt, and the medium gold coloring is unchanging throughout the life of the bloom.

SUTTER'S GOLD. This probably belongs under the blends. However, just as Garden Party serves very nicely as a white rose, Sutter's Gold will serve as a yellow. Its basic color is a deep gold that, in the bud, is overlaid and splotched with cherry red. As the blooms open, however, the red coloration becomes less noticeable and the general effect is of a very large, extremely fragrant yellow rose that, in terms of vigor, behaves more like a pink or red than a yellow. This is a pleasant, easy-going variety that makes a big, robust bush and blooms most freely.

Oranges

True orange and vermilion tones are something new in roses. Whereas a few years ago they were practically unknown, now there are a number of varieties on the market that are so pronouncedly orange that they almost look artificial.

MONTEZUMA. This rose, introduced by Armstrong in 1955, varies in color from a blend of scarlet and orange to a solid, rather dark orange, depending on the season of the year and the temperature. Like other grandifloras, it produces a lot of bloom on a tall, vigorous bush. I have found it highly reliable and hardy. The form of the blooms is excellent, handsome in all stages of development. A spontaneous mutation of Montezuma in Holland produced the variety Floriade, which is much like it but of a lighter color. Either is good.

Tropicana. Unquestionably this is the leading orange rose at present. It is the product of the German plant breeder, Mathau Tantau, who introduced it in Europe in 1960 under the name Super Star. It was introduced in this country two years later as Tropicana, and the following year was an All-America selection. Altogether, this rose has probably won more medals than any other in the history of rosedom. I first grew it in 1960, before it reached the general market, and regard it in a rather special way. It is virtually unique. In color, particularly in cool weather, it reminds me of a well-ripened tangerine. It blooms slightly paler in very hot weather, but whatever the initial color of the bud, this color will persist without fading or change till the bloom wilts. As a cut rose, it is almost without equal. It will last for two weeks in an arrangement if the water is changed regularly.

Under optimum conditions—when the plant is well fed, well watered, and deeply mulched—the bloom of Tropicana will often exceed six inches in diameter. Under nearly any conditions, it flowers freely and with little interruption. It is more resistant to disease than most roses, and shows great winter hardiness. Few roses display better form: it is a natural for exhibition. I find the fragrance, which is pronounced and of a fruity sort, agreeable, though not as exciting as a true damask scent. Tropicana's maternal grandfather was Peace, which may partly explain its many fine qualities. Anyhow, this is a rose that you should have.

COMMAND PERFORMANCE. This rose, a descendant of Tropicana and Hawaii, bears a strong resemblance to Tropicana and was an All-America selection for 1971. To my eye, it differs primarily in color: the backs of the petals have a reddish-orange rather than a true orange cast. In other respects it seems to share most of Tropicana's salient qualities of vigor and generosity, and it carries a similar perfume. Time will tell whether this rose will do as well as Tropicana as a long-term favorite, but I am inclined to give odds that it will.

GYPSY. Ollie Weeks, the California hybridist, has produced a really different rose in Gypsy, with a personality all its own. It has rowdy, pushy manners, demanding and getting your attention, which may partly explain its having been a 1973 All-America selection. The blooms are a deep burnt orange, with the reverse of the petals showing a pinkish-orange shade, quite unusual and charming. The petals are very large and substantial, making a heavy bloom that should be quite resistant to hard rains. As is the case with most roses, the buds are considerably darker than the open flowers. Aside from its color, which will make you blink, the rose is remarkable for the generosity of its bloom, the vigor of its growth habits, and the decorative quality of its foliage, which is as pretty as that of a good holly. It would be hard to go wrong on this one.

Blends

A blend is a rose that displays two or more colors, but is to be distinguished from a bicolor; the latter has one color on the front of the petals and a wholly different color on the reverse.

To my eye, blends are the most subtle and in many ways the most fascinating of roses, so that to make a selection is particularly difficult. I have already mentioned two excellent blends, Garden Party and Sutter's Gold. To select my favorite blend is easy. After that, the choice becomes very hard.

PEACE. This rose was the result of a rather unusual series of crosses performed by a young French hybridist, Francis Meilland, now deceased. Tracing the ancestry of Peace, it appears that Meilland took an orange-red hybrid tea called Charles P. Kilham and crossed it with the Austrian Briar Rose which, you will recall, was the basis of the pernetiana strain of yellow roses. He also crossed Charles P. Kilham with Margaret McGredy, an orange hybrid tea. Seedlings from these two unions were then crossed, and pollen from the resulting hybrid was used to fertilize the yellow hybrid tea, Joanna Hill. (I find it interesting to note that Joanna Hill was the maternal parent both of Peace and Eclipse.) Offhand, I would guess that Meilland was after either a yellow or an orange rose; instead he got a pale creamy-yellow rose, magnificently flushed and tinged with pink and pale cerise tones, a rose that starts in the bud as a deep cream color and gradually deepens and changes as the pink flush spreads through the petals. Here was a rose such as no one had ever seen before. The petals were large and of great substance. The blooms were huge, six inches or more in diameter; the leaves were large, and of a shiny dark green, rather like the foliage of holly; the bush was big, lusty, bursting with energy and vigor; and the huge flowers were borne in unheard-of profusion on fine, strong stems. In all, it had virtually everything but a pronounced perfume.

A dutiful son, Meilland named the rose Mme. A. Meilland for his mother. The Italians called it Gioia (Joy); the Germans prayerfully named it Gloria Dei (Glory of God). The Conard-Pyle Company, which introduced the new rose in 1945 to an America that was licking its wounds after World War II, named it simply Peace, the loveliest name they could think of at the time.

Now and then a really important break occurs in rose hybridizing; Peace represents such a break. Not only has Peace outsold every other variety on the market, it has been used in the breeding of scores and scores of fine new roses, to most of which it has imparted beauty, hardiness, and vigor. I have a hunch that its dash of Austrian Briar blood may account for some of its remarkable qualities. The Eskimos occasionally use a wolf as the sire in breeding huskies; they find that the wild blood puts new life and vigor into the domestic breed. Perhaps something similar took place in the case of Peace.

Strangely, after Peace had been on the market for about fifteen years, mutations began to appear spontaneously in the variety. A plant of Peace would put out a branch bearing blooms that looked very different from the original. Two of these mutations, or "sports," are significant: Chicago Peace and Lucky Piece. Both of these grow and behave in the same way as Peace; both bear blooms that are shaped like those of Peace. Both sports, however, have very highly colored blooms. Chicago Peace has strong pink and cherry tones overlaying a gold base, and no two blooms are ever quite alike; Lucky Piece is similar, except that it often displays orange and vermilion markings. I like both of these sports immensely; they make charming companions for Peace.

GRANADA. Winner of the All-America award for 1964, this hybrid tea will provide more gay, continuous color in the garden than almost any rose I know of. It behaves more like a floribunda, usually bearing clusters of three to five blooms to each stem, and when the plant is in bloom you can hardly find the leaves for the flowers. Like many of the very bright blends—a case in point is the floribunda Circus—there is a great variability in the individual blooms. All, however, display brilliant flushes of pale yellow, nasturtium red, and scarlet. The individual flowers are of medium size; I suppose if one rigorously pinched off the side buds from each cluster, the bush would produce a smaller number of much larger blooms, but the idea is unthinkable. This rose is at its best when it is allowed to bloom without interference, which is the way I managed it in the Municipal Rose Garden. Incidentally, I noticed that visitors to the garden would spot Granada from afar and go straight to it. Granada's enthusiasm about blooming is indicative of unusual plant vigor. As might be expected, this rose is both tough and hardy, an excellent choice for the beginner's rose garden.

TIFFANY. This exquisite pink blend, an All-America selection for 1955, was produced by Robert V. Linquist, who also developed Granada. Since its introduction, it has proven to be an almost universal favorite, both of those gardeners who grow roses merely for their own satisfaction, and those who like to win ribbons at rose shows. After nearly twenty years it still walks off with blue ribbons with remarkable frequency, and probably will continue to do so for a long time, as it has all the requirements of a good exhibition rose: long, strong stems; fine foliage; long, tapering buds opening into large, high-centered blooms; and strong, damask fragrance. The petals are of a warm pink, suffused at the base with gold. Many exhibition roses call for a lot of babying and fussing, but not this one. It makes a good-sized bush of great vigor and hardiness, and seems to do well everywhere.

MEDALLION. I have always had a weakness for roses that show shades of apricot, peach, and buff. This recent blend, an All-America winner for 1973, won me immediately. The basic color is a pinkish apricot or peach, suffused at the base of each petal with clear, light gold. The form of the blooms is impeccable, whether in the bud or when fully open; and when they do open, they frequently reach seven inches in diameter. All this on a tall, handsome bush that grows with great vigor. I predict a long success for this rose.

LADY ELGIN. To me, a well-grown bloom of this rose is incomparable. The base color of the petals is a deep yellow or orange, very subtly tinged with tints of apricot and red. One of its grandparents was Peace, which may help to account for the great size and substance of the blooms. This is not a rose to be grown lightly: it will not tolerate neglect. However, if you are willing to devote a lot of time to tending, cultivating, and spraying Lady Elgin, you will find her fascinating.

Bicolors

CONDESA DE SASTAGO. An old favorite that has been on the market since 1932, the same year that witnessed the introduction of Eclipse, this rose is primarily distinguished by its free-blooming characteristics and easygoing nature. Not at all fussy, it grows lustily, making a tall bushy plant, and bears quantities of very brightly colored blooms. This is not a rose for cutting; the stems are too short to be effective in arrangements. Rather, it is best grown as a display rose to give a big splash of color. The colors themselves are extremely bright: a deep watermelon pink on the front of the petals with the reverse in gold. In cool weather the pink may deepen to scarlet or Oriental red. Don't plant it adjacent to pale pinks or delicate blends. It will look better along with reds or yellows, or in contrast to a white variety. In any case, put it in the back row, for it is tall growing. This is quite a fragrant rose, by the way.

COLORAMA. This rose, a recent introduction from Conard-Pyle, is rather like Condesa de Sastago in general appearance. Like the latter, the reverse of the petals is bright gold, but the front of the petals is watermelon pink at the top and gold at the base. It is too early in this rose's career to predict whether it will have as long a popularity as Condesa de Sastago, but it promises to be a very satisfactory addition to the rose garden. For one thing, it grows with a little less abandon than the Condesa, which is always shouldering other roses to one side, and the blooms come on long, strong stems, excellent for cutting and arranging. In cool weather the blooms of

Colorama deepen in color, the pink becoming a Chinese red. The fragrance of the rose, which is of the tea sort, is relatively slight, a minor fault. I think Colorama is most attractive when it is fully open. It has a great many —forty to fifty—very large petals, and these open in an open cupped shape to display the very prominent gold stamens. I find this rose much to my taste.

Lavenders

I take back everything I have ever said or thought about lavender hybrid teas. Despite their beauty of form and their fragrance, most of these roses depress me and make me start thinking about when I am going to die and what people will say about me at my funeral. But there is a new one, of such perfection of form and color that I think it deserves a place in every rose garden.

HEIRLOOM. This rose, introduced by Jackson & Perkins, is colored a deep lilac, unlike any other rose I have ever seen. The blooms are large and finely formed, with a good tight center, which makes them attractive in all stages. As is true with most roses, the buds are deeper in color than the open blooms; in the case of Heirloom they are purple. There is nothing bashful about Heirloom; it blooms very generously on a tall, vigorous plant, reaching a height of four feet or more, with a good spread to the branches. And the perfume is magnificent.

So much for my list of favorite hybrid teas and grandifloras. It is admittedly incomplete, and, of course, it unabashedly reflects my own personal likes and dislikes.

It omits many handsome and potentially superior roses that have newly reached the market. Five years from now, when these roses will have had a chance to prove their worth, my list may be radically different.

In passing, I have to say that I mourn the disappearance of many fine roses that as recently as five years ago were readily obtainable from U.S. dealers. There was, for example, Orange Flame, which I considered to be equal and in some ways superior to Tropicana. And there was Coronado, my favorite red and gold bicolor, which outperformed most roses in my garden and was quite unexcelled for cutting. (If you ever run across one, buy it.) Several factors have contributed to roses being dropped from the market. For one thing, a number of nurseries that used to produce quantities of introductions every year have gone out of business. The nursery business, like the auto industry, has boiled down to three or four giants, and these companies, for purely economic reasons, find it essential to stop raising most of the older varieties in favor of being able to present the newer roses. It makes excellent business sense, but it is rather sad.

For purposes of general information, and for easy reference, I am including in Appendix A a much longer list of reliable hybrid teas and grandifloras that I consider worthy of note. Those marked with an asterisk are All-America winners.

I V

Choice Floribundas

FLORIBUNDAS, as I indicated earlier, are relatively new to the rose garden; most of the major improvements in the type have taken place since 1940. Progress in developing floribundas has been phenomenal. One could now plant an entire rose garden in floribundas, with highly satisfactory results. In terms of stature, bloom form, color, and fragrance, virtually every characteristic of hybrid teas may now be found in floribundas.

When I was asked to design the layout and plantings of the Clarksville Municipal Rose Garden, I was concerned with achieving two principal results. First, I wanted to display a major collection of the best modern hybrid teas, so that visitors on foot could see these fine flowers at their best. Second, I wanted to create a dazzling display of color that would stop passing motorists and bring them on foot into the garden. To attain this second result, I used massed plantings of floribundas, prominently placed in the front of the garden, where they would attract the most attention from the street.

The result was all I could have hoped for. Of all the varieties of roses in the garden, the ones that prompted the most questions from visitors were floribundas.

I have seldom grown a floribunda that I disliked; nearly every one of them has had the characteristics of hardiness, vigor, and generosity of bloom that set floribundas apart from most other roses. Nevertheless, there have been some for which I have entertained a particular affection, and these I propose to describe to you. If a large proportion of them happen to have been produced by Gene Boerner, this should occasion no surprise. More than any other plant breeder, Boerner was responsible, either directly or indirectly, for the perfection of the floribunda type. Few men have left the world a more charming legacy.

Reds

Fire King. An All-America selection, this rose is as bright and arresting as a stoplight. The color is a vivid Chinese red, a sort of scarlet-vermilion mixture, unrelieved and unchanging. The plant is tall and well branched, often reaching a height of four feet with a proportionate spread. The individual blooms are of great substance, having about fifty petals, and consequently are long lasting, whether on the plant or when cut. Few floribundas are as bright or as exciting as this one.

Europeana. Another All-America winner, this relatively short, compact variety distinguishes itself for its remarkable profusion of bloom. The flowers are produced in immense sprays, fifteen or twenty to a cluster, and are of a brilliant medium to dark red. The fully open bloom, which is lightly cupped, displays handsome golden stamens. While it is seldom out of bloom, the foliage alone is attractive enough to warrant a place for Europeana in the garden: large, dark green, glossy leaves, with the new growth a copper red, like the leaves of a Japanese maple.

LILI MARLENE. Like Europeana, this rose has relatively few petals and opens to a semicupped form, making a very bright display of its golden stamens. What distinguishes it is its deep, unvarying crimson color, in cool weather nearly as dark as that of Oklahoma. The buds, in fact, are practically black. It blooms in very large sprays and keeps going almost without interruption all through the season, making a most effective splash of color. I grew it in front of a row of white roses—Ivory Fashion, I believe—and it was utterly lovely. Too bad it has grown a little hard to find.

GARNETTE. Originally a greenhouse rose grown for small corsages and boutonnieres, this rose had a successful career under glass before people realized it was also a good garden rose. It makes a short, compact bush, covered with very small, intensely dark red blooms, something like those of an old-fashioned rambler. One peculiarity of Garnette is how long the blooms stay good on the plant before they begin to fade. I've known them to last two weeks in mild weather. This rose, incidentally, has produced a distinguished line of progeny, and has greatly contributed to developing the modern floribunda. Because of its short stature and tidy growth habits, Garnette is fine for low borders and edgings, to set off taller roses or to edge a walk.

Oranges

GINGER. Nearly everything about Ginger is different and distinctive. The plant doesn't look like other rose bushes, having nearly thornless canes of a coppery color, most unusual and attractive. The blooms, which are about four inches in diameter, are of a vivid orange color and are borne in great profusion. Of the floribundas planted in the Municipal Rose Garden, Ginger always excited special interest from visitors, partly because of its remarkable generosity of bloom, partly by reason of its brilliant coloration.

I first grew Ginger as a test rose about two years before its general introduction in 1962. Gene Boerner was particularly proud of this rose, and with justice. Its ancestry is distinguished, including Spartan, Garnette, and a double cross of Crimson Glory. Offhand I can't think of a better floribunda, nor one more generally useful. If you grow it, give it plenty of room, as it makes a lusty, tall bush.

SPARTAN. Of almost the same color as Ginger, Spartan differs from it principally in having thorny, green canes and blooms of a more conventional urn shape. It also makes an unusually large bush, about four feet tall in temperate regions. In Florida I have seen it stand six feet tall. Spartan is another Boerner rose, and served as the male parent of Ginger. I have absolutely no reservations about this rose.

BAHIA. A brand-new floribunda, and a 1974 All-America selection, this rose fills a needed place for a low-growing orange floribunda. The blooms vary from clear orange to burnt orange, open into cupped flowers about two inches in diameter, and quite obscure the foliage when flowering is at its height. The foliage, by the way, is unusually attractive. Its relatively low-growing habit, which can be a real asset in a floribunda, suits this rose for massing in front of tall-growing hybrid teas, or for use in low hedges and borders for walks. It would be magnificent if it were planted in front of a rose like Blanche Mallerin, White Masterpiece, or Saratoga.

Pinks

GENE BOERNER. Posthumously introduced and named in honor of its breeder, this pink floribunda won All-America honors in 1969. Floribundas tend to take three principal forms, depending, I think, on whether they take after the polyantha side of their ancestry, or after the hybrid tea parentage. Those that resemble their polyantha heritage, such as Lili Marlene and Europeana, either tend to be only semidouble and open up flat or cupped, with a prominent display of stamens; or to make very tight, rounded blooms with a great many small petals, somewhat after the fashion of rambler roses; examples of the latter would be Garnette and China Doll. Those that take after their hybrid tea ancestors make blooms that have the classic urn shape in the bud and open to relatively tight, high-centered flowers. These floribundas look like smaller editions of the familiar hybrid teas. Typical examples of this type of floribunda would be Spartan, Fashion, and Saratoga. Gene Boerner is of the last type, and produces great quantities of small medium-pink blooms of hybrid-tea form on a medium-sized bush. Where Europeana or China Doll, for example, may produce fifteen or twenty blooms in a single cluster, Gene Boerner and most of the other floribundas of its type may produce five to seven.

It is largely a question of what you want in a rose. For mass effect, the polyantha type of floribunda is best. For individual bloom quality with a reasonable display of color, choose the hybrid-tea type.

I think you will like Gene Boerner: the rose has much to offer, and nothing that I know of to fault. I do, however, mourn two of its relatives that I grew and loved, Gay Princess and Bonnie Pink. Both have become very difficult to find; both were superb floribundas of the hybrid-tea type.

FASHION. Strictly speaking, this belongs with the blends, for the base color, a light pink, is tinged with shades of peach, and there may also be a touch of gold as well. This Boerner rose has been going strong since its introduction in 1949, and it has won many awards, including the All-America in 1950. Whatever its official color classification, the general effect is that of a pink rose, and a mighty fine one. The bush grows tall and broad, needing plenty of room and a back row position. The blooms, of the hybrid-tea type, open to nearly four inches in diameter. This is one of the few floribundas of its period to survive. I would recommend it most highly.

CHINA DOLL. Strictly speaking a polyantha, but marketed as a floribunda, this rose produces bright pink blooms that nearly cover the plant. The blooms themselves are tight and rounded, with very small petals closely set, and resemble the flowers of a rambler. This is definitely a dwarf variety, seldom getting more than eighteen inches tall. Because of its low stature and generous, almost continuous bloom, it is exceptionally useful as a border or hedging plant. China Doll, produced by Walter Lammerts, has been on the market since 1946, and shows every indication of maintaining its popularity for a long time to come.

Yellows

SPANISH SUN. Of the yellow floribundas that I have seen, this definitely impresses me the most. The flowers are a deep, pure gold and seem little inclined to grow pale in hot sunshine, a fault of many yellow roses. The form is that of a small hybrid tea about three inches in diameter, exquisite from bud to fully open bloom. The plant blooms both singly and in small clusters, and makes long stems, fine for cutting. The height of the bush is moderate, around two feet, lending itself to planting in the front of the bed. Best of all, this rose has a really powerful damask fragrance. I can't see how you could go wrong with it.

GOLD CUP. Another fragrant yellow floribunda, Gold Cup has been popular since its introduction in 1957. It is of the hybrid-tea type with larger than usual blooms for a floribunda. Its cupped flowers, when fully open, often exceed four inches in diameter. Bloom is generous on a reasonably tall plant, and enough flowers are borne singly to make it a useful source of cut flowers. Gold Cup's All-America award was well deserved.

Whites

If my list of outstanding yellow floribundas seemed small, it is because there are relatively few good yellows on the market. The same is true of white floribundas. Why it should be I do not know, but white and yellow roses are notably cantankerous, temperamental, and frustrating in comparison with other colors. Exceptions to the rule are a gardener's delight.

IVORY FASHION. A perfectly exquisite semidouble rose of pale ivory, this floribunda, like Lili Marlene and Europeana, is most attractive when the bloom is wide open and displays its stamens. One of the handsomest beds in the Municipal Rose Garden was planted with Ivory Fashion and Lili Marlene. The two roses, quite similar in form, made a delightful color contrast.

Unlike many white roses, Ivory Fashion is hardy and reliable, blooms freely, and seldom presents any problems. These facts being indisputable, it seems strange to me that few rose nurseries still handle it, offering Saratoga instead. Since the two are wholly different, I can't regard the substitution as reasonable. I should like to see a planting of Ivory Fashion and Europeana; they should complement each other perfectly.

SARATOGA. This great floribunda bears hybrid-tea type blooms that closely resemble gardenias—the whitest of white, with a waxy texture. The buds, however, start off as a delicate ivory. The combination is lovely, both in arrangements and on the bush.

Like Ivory Fashion, Saratoga is a Boerner rose, and won an All-America award in 1964. It makes a good, upright bush about three feet tall, bears generously, and generally behaves like a lady. In addition to all its other attractive qualities, Saratoga is fragrant.

Lavenders

ANGEL FACE. All of my reservations and prejudices about lavender floribunda roses went by the board the first time I ever grew Angel Face. I find this rose enchanting. The blooms are of a deep lavender, flushed on the edges of the petals with ruby red, and shaped like a hybrid tea. At no point from tight bud to fully open flower is the form unpleasing. When the bloom is wide open it forms a shallow cup, with a splendid display of gold stamens. Many lavender roses tend to fade badly in hot sun, as the bloom opens, but not this one. And the perfume is a delight, a solid damask scent.

The bush is well branched and of moderate size, about two feet tall, with fine, dark, glossy leaves. Altogether a great rose, which must have gratified Swim & Weeks, who hybridized it and won an All-America award in 1969 for their efforts.

If there are other really outstanding lavender floribundas, I don't know of them.

Blends

There have been quantities of good blends among floribundas, many of which, like Bellina and Golden Slippers and Little Darling, have either wholly or nearly disappeared from the market, replaced by newer varieties.

With very few exceptions, the blends that I have grown have delighted me. Nearly all of them have been gay and generous, contributing mightily to garden color, and producing exceptionally attractive blooms for cutting. A few of my old favorites are still available, and happily, some exceptionally fine new ones have recently been introduced.

APRICOT NECTAR. If I could grow only one floribunda blend, it would be this one. One of Gene Boerner's last achievements before his death, this rose is quite distinctive. It bears a majority of its blooms singly, on good long stems and in great profusion. Shaped like fine hybrid teas, the blooms open to as much as five inches in diameter, and give off a magnificent damask scent. The color is hard to describe, a sort of pale, slightly pinkish apricot, deepening pronouncedly in the center of the bloom. The bush is rather tall, three feet or more, and well proportioned, with dark, glossy leaves. Definitely not a border rose, Apricot Nectar is better planted along with hybrid teas of moderate height, in which company it will more than hold its own. Few roses have better deserved the All-America award that this one received in 1966.

RED GOLD. An Irish rose from Dickson's in Northern Ireland, Red Gold was introduced in this country by Jackson & Perkins, and won the All-America for 1971. And a better rose it would be hard to find, both for the form of the blooms and their brilliant coloration. The base color of the petals is an orange-gold, with the tips of the petals flushed with a light red that turns to a fairly dark cerise. The edges of the petals are rolled back, a form that I always think imparts a special look of solidity to the blooms. The general shape of the flowers is that of a small hybrid tea, and the medium-tall plant bears them profusely. I like everything about this rose, and I would recommend it highly.

CIRCUS. This is a rose that can't make up its mind, seldom producing two blooms exactly alike. The flowers have a base color of light gold, and the petals are overlaid with various tints of pink, salmon, and scarlet in bewildering variety. Bloom is unusually heavy, and is carried in large trusses of twenty or so.

This rose was produced by Herb Swim and was introduced by Armstrong Nurseries, which promptly received an All-America for it in 1956. Ever since, it has been going great guns. Personally I don't care for it, but I must be wrong, for nearly everyone else seems to be crazy about it. You probably will be, too. In any case, it will grow lustily nearly anywhere it is planted, and can be relied on to stay in flower almost continuously. Incidentally, this is one floribunda that is particularly well suited to use as a hedge, as it makes a compact bush of moderate height.

FABERGÉ. This is an enchanting new floribunda of the hybrid-tea sort, with blooms shaped much like those of Gene Boerner. The flowers start off in the bud as pink shaded with coral, and open to a deeper pink tinged with yellow. The combination reminds me of a lighter-than-usual bloom of Tiffany. Aside from being very free-blooming, this rose has a nice habit of bearing many of its blooms one to a stem, which makes them exceptionally good for cutting. The plant itself is of medium height, perhaps thirty inches tall, with a good spread, and the foliage is quite handsome. This one should be a winner.

I could add a number of other fine floribundas to this list, but those I have mentioned should suffice to give you an idea of how versatile and delightful floribundas can be. You will find an expanded list of floribundas in Appendix B (page 219).

V

Choice Climbers

In comparison with the number of varieties of hybrid teas on the market, the rose grower has relatively little choice in the selection of climbers. Even the largest nurseries in the United States stock fewer than a score of varieties. And those that are stocked will almost all be either large-flowered, everblooming climbers or climbing forms of hybrid teas. Almost gone from the American market are the ramblers and the nonrecurrent large-flowered climbers that were so common a few decades ago. A few, such as Dorothy Perkins, Paul's Scarlet, and Silver Moon are still fairly commonly seen on fences and trellises in older neighborhoods, but most of them, I suspect, have been grown from rooted cuttings started under mason jars.

On the whole, I believe the modern preference in climbers is justified. Nearly all of the better modern climbers bear flowers that are practically indistinguishable from those of the best hybrid teas and floribundas and produce them by the hundreds. The older climbers and ramblers, with a few exceptions, produce vast quantities of individual blooms, but the flowers themselves lack the form and refinement of bush roses. Most modern climbers can be relied upon for an immense initial burst of bloom followed all season by smaller but still impressive repeat performances. The older climbers, on the other hand, tend to bloom only once and then quit for the entire year. Really, you get much more for your money from the modern climbers.

Another difference that distinguishes the modern from the old climbers and ramblers is the size of the plant. Most of the older varieties grow to very considerable size: City of York, for example, still one of the finest white climbing roses, will put out individual canes measuring ten or twelve feet, so that a single bush may spread over more than twenty feet of fence or trellis; Silver Moon and Dorothy Perkins will cover just about as much territory. Such enthusiastic growth habits were more welcome in the early years of this century, when lots and houses tended to be large, than in this day of smaller houses and still smaller yards. Most modern climbers, by comparison, have a spread of about six feet and a height of from five to eight feet.

Because it always takes an exception to prove a rule, I should point out that the most popular of all modern climbers, Blaze, grows with nearly as much abandon as any of the old climbers. I've seen it reach a height of nearly twelve feet and break down a fairly sturdy trellis with the weight of its flowers and branches.

Here are a few climbing roses that should appeal to most gardeners.

Reds

BLAZE. While there is some dispute about the origin of this remarkable climber, it appears to have been hybridized by one Joseph W. Kallay of Painesville, Ohio. If Mr. Kallay developed any other noteworthy roses, none of the horticultural reference books at my disposal so notes. In any case, Blaze was introduced in 1932 by Jackson & Perkins; it has been going strong ever since. The maternal parent of Blaze is said to have been Paul's Scarlet Climber, a famous old rose that it greatly resembles. Both have rather loose, raggedy blooms of a brilliant scarlet color, about two inches in diameter, and borne in almost unbelievable profusion. Blaze makes a rather larger plant than Paul's Scarlet and tends to be considerably more recurrent. However, it is not wholly safe to generalize. There are, apparently, several strains of Blaze on the market, some of which are definitely superior to the others. The better strains of Blaze bloom heavily in early summer and then repeat rather weakly on a monthly basis until the first frosts. The less desirable strains tend to bloom only once a season. As far as I know, the only way to be sure of getting one of the better strains is to order from one of the major rose nurseries that cannot afford to carry anything less than the best.

RED EMPRESS. A big, lusty plant with big red blooms like those of a good hybrid tea, this rose is a lovely sight in bloom. Like Blaze, it makes a very large bush and requires strong support. It is quite strongly recurrent, and can be counted on to show considerable color all season.

DON JUAN. This is another big red climber, not quite as rampant as Blaze or Red Empress, but still making a very impressive bush. It produces very strong, stiff canes, and so can stand with only minimal support, such as a post to which to tie the main trunk. The blooms are very large, around five inches in diameter, have a deep, crimson color and a strong, old-rose fragrance. Like Red Empress, Don Juan makes an excellent source of cut flowers, since it blooms almost continuously and carries its flowers singly on good stems.

Incidentally, Don Juan, so I am assured by Mr. B. J. Nelson of Nelson's Florida Roses, the principal supplier of roses to Florida, is about the only reliable climber in central Florida, and the only variety that he recommends without reservation.

Pinks

NEW DAWN. I suspect that this is the most widely planted pink climber in the United States. To me, its principal attraction is its color, an apple-blossom pink of great delicacy and purity. The individual blooms are of medium size and come in large trusses. After the first burst of blooms the plant flowers more sparingly, but almost continuously. The growth habit of New Dawn lends it to training on fences particularly well, since the canes are unusually long and not excessively stiff. Incidentally, the more nearly horizontally you can make the canes grow, the better they will flower, particularly if you take the trouble to cut the lateral shoots back to about four eyes each.

BLOSSOMTIME. A descendant of New Dawn, Blossomtime makes a much more moderate bush and bears somewhat larger flowers in a two-tone arrangement of dark and light pink. Otherwise, the two climbers behave in much the same way. However, where New Dawn has very little fragrance, Blossomtime is unusually sweet. For a small property, this would be an excellent choice.

RHONDA. A pink climber of recent introduction, this is quite different from either New Dawn or Blossomtime. Its growth and blooming characteristics are similar to those of Don Juan. The bush grows to a height of about eight feet and is stiff enough to stand with very little support. Unlike many climbers, it will usually bloom in its first year; most don't get around to this till the second year. The blooms are of hybrid-tea form, are carried on fine cutting stems, and are of a light pink with a coral blush, large and handsome. In common with the better modern climbers, this rose blooms continuously all through the season.

DR. J. H. NICOLAS. Named for the hybridist who developed Eclipse as well as many other, lesser roses, this climber has been popular since its introduction in 1940, and is likely to continue indefinitely. The bush grows to about eight feet in height and bears great quantities of very double, very fragrant, large pink blooms in small clusters of two or three.

Corals and Oranges

CORAL DAWN. Another descendant of New Dawn, this rose makes a large climber, which may go to a height of twelve feet, and consequently should be given considerable support. The blooms are large, resembling those of hybrid teas, and vary from coral to medium pink. The flowers come in clusters of three to twenty, giving a spectacular effect, but making the rose less desirable for cutting than some others. Still, it has a nice fragrance, and blooms with great regularity all season. A good rose, particularly for large properties.

CLIMBING SPARTAN. A sport of the earlier introduced floribunda, this climber has all of the virtues that have made Spartan so popular. For me, it quickly attained a height of about six feet, grew without support, and produced great quantities of burnt-orange blooms, three or four inches in diameter, of excellent form and fine fragrance. The plant tends to bloom in clusters of three or more, but I also discovered that a little judicious disbudding would produce fine single blooms on long stems, perfect for cutting. My observation was that the plant seldom seemed to slow down its blooming, and was almost never without color during the growing season.

One important aspect of this rose needs mention. Whereas many climbing forms of hybrid teas make a spectacular and very satisfying display of blooms, they are very susceptible to winter damage and may be killed by sudden spells of low temperatures. Climbing Spartan, on the other hand, inherits the great hardiness that characterizes the floribunda, and is inclined to shrug off low temperatures, just as it tends to make light of fungus infections. This is one I would recommend without qualms.

KASSEL. This rose, which I have described at some length in Chapter II under shrub roses, needs mention here. You will find it hard to obtain, and will have to send off to a specialist in rare roses to get a specimen, but it will be well worth your trouble. This rose, which bears quantities of small, burnt-orange blooms of classic hybrid-tea form, can be used either as a shrub or climber. I put it to the latter use. It made a sturdy bush about eight feet tall, bloomed all season, and seemed to ignore black spot and insects. Why American growers largely ignore it, I have no idea.

Yellows

GOLDEN SHOWERS. This rose, like its half-sister Climbing High Noon, is one of the few climbers to receive an All-America award. Golden Showers has much to recommend it: constant, generous bloom; large, slightly scented flowers; a tendency to bear singly rather than in clusters; and a sturdy, upright habit of growth that largely obviates the need for support. A production of Walter Lammerts, it won an All-America in 1957, which must have surprised Lammerts, for he had previously won the same award for Climbing High Noon in 1948. The only fault I can find with Golden Showers is that a combination of strong sunshine and high temperatures will cause the bloom to fade to an uninspiring ivory shade. However, this is not a serious fault, but one that can be easily overlooked in view of its many signal virtues. This rose would make a lovely companion for Don Juan.

CLIMBING HIGH NOON. This rose is a cross between Soeur Thérèse and Captain Thomas, whereas Golden Showers is a cross between Charlotte Armstrong and Captain Thomas. The maternal parent in each case was a hybrid tea, whereas the father was a climber. As might be expected, Climbing High Noon is much like Golden Showers. I think it holds its color a little better than Golden Showers and grows a little more vigorously; at times, also, it will show a hint of pink tones in the yellow. Either of these roses would be a good choice.

ROYAL GOLD. The main difference between this rose and the two previously described is that Royal Gold bears considerably larger blooms in small clusters and makes a somewhat smaller bush, between five and seven feet in height. The color is a medium gold, which holds up well in hot weather. One virtue of this rose is that, unlike many climbers, it almost always blooms the year it is planted.

Whites

CLIMBING CITY OF YORK. Good white climbing roses are rare. This one was introduced in 1945, and has become difficult to locate. Nevertheless, I think it is worth looking for: in spite of several disadvantages, the most serious being that it blooms only once a year, I would still rate it as the most spectacular of white climbers. Its semidouble blooms are high centered and exquisitely formed, particularly in the half-open stage. The color is a creamy ivory, indescribably lovely. These perfect little blooms are borne in large clusters. Properly grown, City of York virtually drowns itself in a sea of blooms.

This is a splendid fence rose. The canes are rather lax and can easily be trained to a horizontal position. In this attitude, it will flower particularly heavily, a characteristic of most climbers. Try growing it along with New Dawn or Blaze for a really spectacular effect.

CLIMBING WHITE DAWN. The University of Minnesota has for many years been concerned with developing hardy roses that will withstand the rigors of northern winters. White Dawn is one of the roses they have produced with this purpose in mind. The maternal parent was New Dawn, while the hybrid tea Lili Pons was the paternal parent. Tracing the ancestry of Lili Pons back several generations, I come upon *R. wichuraiana* blood. This particular Asiatic species keeps cropping up in the pedigrees of the most famous old climbers and ramblers, and it may account for White Dawn's vigor.

In any case, White Dawn makes a medium-sized bush and bears quantities of large, pure white, glossy blooms all season long. I'm sure you will like it.

So much for the climbers. Readers who have some acquaintance with rose growing may wonder why I have made no mention of the climbing forms of hybrid teas, such as Climbing Peace and Climbing Crimson Glory. There is even a Climbing Tropicana. My feelings about these roses are mixed. When one of them succeeds, it is about as glorious a sight as can be imagined. Often the climbing forms produce larger and better blooms than the bush form of the same rose, and bear them by the hundreds on plants six or eight feet tall. The catch is that most climbing hybrid teas are woefully tender: an unexpected early freeze in the fall, before the canes of the plant have had time to go dormant and harden up, can—and frequently does—kill back the entire top of the bush, and may take the bud union as well.

Now, when you plant a climbing hybrid tea, the bush will almost always spend the first season making canes, and will not flower until the second year, when it will do so on the canes produced in the first year. A single freeze-back, therefore, will set the rose back two seasons, even if it doesn't kill it. All of this can be utterly maddening.

If you live in a relatively mild climate area where untimely fall freezes are very rare, then you would do well to try some of these climbing hybrid teas. They will reward you bountifully in the second year after planting, and in succeeding years with great regularity.

I would offer one suggestion. Both Climbing Peace and Climbing Crimson Glory are out of patent and can be legally reproduced from cuttings. In my experience, both of them do superlatively well on their own roots. Consequently, if you can get some cuttings of these roses and root your own plants, you can provide yourself with a margin of safety. With an own-root bush, even if the whole top is frozen to the ground, the roots will usually push up a new top for you, which should flower again in the second year.

These reservations about climbing forms of hybrid teas do not apply to the climbing forms of floribundas, several of which are now on the market. Floribundas don't seem to be bothered much by cold snaps.

Appendix C (page 222) lists a number of good climbers not described in this chapter.

VI

Buying Rose Bushes

I'M SURE your first reaction to the heading of this chapter was that the procedure is self-evident and does not warrant discussion. Unfortunately, this is a common notion that causes a lot of disappointment to gardeners every year. There is more to buying roses than merely answering an advertisement from a gardening magazine or picking up a few plants downtown. Not all dealers in roses are honest. And many genuinely honest dealers, particularly retailers, unwittingly handle inferior rose plants or ruin good plants before they are sold. In either case, it is the customer who suffers.

To understand all the whys and wherefores and don'ts of rose buying, you have to know something about how roses are handled at the nursery where the plants are grown, and how they are prepared for sale to the customer.

As a buyer of rose plants, you have four choices open to you:

1. You can purchase bare-root, dormant rose bushes by mail from a nursery that grows them.

2. You can buy from a local dealer bare-root roses whose roots are packed in damp moss or sawdust, and whose tops may or may not be waxed.

3. You can buy from a local dealer roses that have been potted and shipped in some kind of patent container permitting the roots to be kept in soil.

4. Or finally, you can buy roses that have been locally potted in large cans of soil.

Of these four alternatives, which is likely to prove most generally satisfactory to the home gardener? To find out, let us see how these roses are made ready for sale.

Up to a certain point, all rose bushes are prepared in much the same way. The rose varieties—Peace or Crimson Glory or Charlotte Armstrong or Tropicana or whatnot—are bud-grafted ("budded") to the roots of a hardy understock, and the resulting plants are grown for from two to three years in big fields like so much corn. (Why and how roses are bud-grafted will be discussed in later chapters.)

In the fall, about the time that growth naturally slows down, the rose bushes are dug by special machines. The leaves are removed from the tops, and the canes are pruned back moderately so as to make them more manageable. Then the tops are tied together with string and the bushes sorted according to the size and number of the canes. The Jumbo and No. 1 plants are all that the better nurseries offer for sale, the No. 1 being the large, standard-sized bushes. Smaller plants, the 1½ size and the really midget No. 2 size, are sorted and set aside. Plants of a single variety are done up in bundles of a convenient number and the plants stored in labeled bins in specially designed storage vaults, where the temperature is kept at a uniform low of about 34° F., and the humidity is controlled to prevent the bushes from becoming desiccated. Under these conditions, despite the fact that the roots are bare and exposed to the air, the plants will stay dormant and will not be impaired in vitality for many months.

Sometime in the course of handling the bushes, either when putting them in storage or when removing them for sale, the roots are inspected, and any that have been broken or damaged, or that are excessively long, are shortened.

Those nurseries that sell directly to individual mail-order customers remove roses from cold storage at planting time, either late in the fall or in the early spring, encase the bushes in a moisture-retaining plastic bag (often with damp moss around the roots), pack them in boxes, and ship them. Better than nine times out of ten, the bushes arrive at their destination in excellent condition, ready to plant.

Nurseries that sell roses to retail sources for resale to individual customers have to make special provisions to assure that the bushes will not die while they are waiting to be sold. By far the commonest way of doing this is to fold the roots of each plant into a compact bundle, put wet moss or sawdust around them, cover the roots with an airtight plastic bag, and then encase the whole base of the plant in a fancy wrapper, usually with a full-color picture of the bloom to tempt the customer. The tops are usually dipped in warm molten wax, which is intended to keep the canes from drying out. A few firms, however, merely prune the tops way back to the hard wood near the base of the canes, which is less likely to lose moisture than the softer wood higher up on the canes. These packaged roses are then held in cold storage until a month or so before rose-planting time, when they are sent to retail dealers: variety stores, hardware stores, garden centers, and supermarkets.

A few nurseries offer rose bushes already planted in soil in a special container. While there is some variation in the containers, the upper part usually forms a sort of protective cage to hold the top of the bush, while the lower end is designed to hold the roots in moist earth and to retain the moisture for a long time.

Finally, local retailers often have roses potted in big tin cans of soil. Some obtain bare-root roses directly from nurseries and pot them up immediately upon arrival; others only pot up leftover packaged roses, so as to save them when the rose-selling season begins to wane. Some also purchase tin-can-potted roses, ready to sell.

Of the four sorts of rose bushes available to the prospective customer, which is most desirable?

Personally, I prefer bare-root roses shipped to me by a nursery that I know and can trust. Next, I would choose unwaxed packaged rose bushes bought early, as soon as possible after they had been received by the local retailer. Container roses, whether potted at the nursery or by the local retailer, I would buy only as a last resort.

Rose bushes held in cold storage at the nurseries are in a state of dormancy, like that of a tree in winter. So long as the cool, moist conditions of the storage vault are maintained, the bushes will not begin to sprout or otherwise break dormancy. However, as soon as the bushes are removed from the storage vaults and subjected to higher temperatures, they begin to "wake up." To come completely out of dormancy takes a rose bush quite a while. In the case of bare-root plants shipped directly to the customer (averaging five or six days in transit), the first premonitory signs of awakening will usually be noticeable when the plants arrive at their destination. The eyes on the canes will be swollen and red, and toward the tops of the canes a few eyes will have pushed out short pointed shoots from which branches will later grow.

In this condition, a rose is ready to grow and receptive to planting. All it needs is to have its roots soaked in water overnight, in case any of them have become desiccated, and it will then be ready to set in the ground. None of the strength of the plant will have been expended in making branches and leaves; all of the starches and sugars stored in the stems and base of the bush during its previous summer of growth will be available to feed the new growth until the roots can resume their task of feeding the plant and the new leaves can begin their magic of turning carbon dioxide from the atmosphere into more starches and sugars.

For these various reasons, I prefer to order bare-root roses from the nurseries that grow them. Not only does one have a wide selection of varieties from which to choose, far more than any garden center can carry, but the plants are guaranteed to be viable. Nurseries can confidently guarantee their rose bushes. The parcel post service is usually quite reliable, and few claims are made against the nurseries. During the several years that I acted as rosarian for the Clarksville Municipal Rose Garden, I ordered and supervised the planting of over seven hundred rose bushes, all obtained as bare-root plants from the nurseries that grew them. In all, only twelve bushes failed to grow, and these were replaced at no charge.

What of bare-root packaged roses, such as are sold in retail outlets? When these rose bushes reach the retailer, they are in a healthy condition, ready for planting. Those that have had their tops waxed have, in some measure, suffered violation: wax on the stems of growing plants is unnatural. In my experience, waxed rose plants often suffer cane damage, particularly during very hot weather. I don't pretend to understand all the details of plant physiology that are probably involved; all I know is that I have found that the waxed canes usually die back and have to be removed, and although the plants make replacement canes, I cannot regard the loss of wood as particularly desirable. In cool areas, waxed plants might be more satisfactory. As for the packaged plants that have unwaxed, heavily pruned tops, I have had reasonably good results from them. Provided they are fresh, and have been properly handled by the retailer, I consider them about as good a risk as bare-root plants shipped directly from the nursery.

Unfortunately, most dealers are ignorant of the needs of these packaged roses. They stand them prominently in front of the store on racks in full sunshine. Or they stand them up in boxes and keep them on counters in steam-heated stores. In either case, the roses, having been awakened from dormancy by the rise in temperature, promptly begin to put out sprouts, which turn into leafy branches. As the roses remain unsold, desiccation starts in the canes; they begin to have a wrinkled look, turning from a healthy green or russet red to an unhealthy brown. About this time, the dealer, seeing his unsold stock of rose plants going begging, puts them on sale at half price. Those that he can't sell he may open, cram the folded roots into No. 10 cans full of soil, and mark "potted roses"; the price tag is customarily fifty cents higher than the original, unreduced price of the rose bushes.

I know many people who deliberately wait until the local dealers in packaged roses put their plants on sale before they buy. I have seen clerks point with confidence to the luxurious, leafy tops of their half-dead rose plants to reassure doubtful customers.

A packaged rose plant that has sat about in a warm store till the top has broken into leaves is in about as good a condition of health as a college student who has been sitting up nights cramming for examinations on a regime of cigarettes, black coffee, and Benzedrine, for the plant has been subjected to a rather similar ordeal. The new canes and leaves have been produced at the expense of the starches and sugars previously stored in the original canes, which are now depleted. The roots and canes are also largely depleted of water, since this moisture has gone into the new growth and the plant has had no way of restoring its moisture balance.

It is probably no coincidence that those people who stated to me that they "can't grow roses" had almost all bought packaged roses on sale at reduced prices.

What about container-shipped roses? In general, these are healthy plants when they reach the customer, even if they are bought rather late in the season. The instructions accompanying them direct the customer to remove the plant with its root-ball intact and replant it in a hole the size of the container. Theoretically, then, the bush should keep growing as it has been doing in the container and be none the worse for the move.

The only fault I have to find with container-shipped plants is that they have too small a root system. Obviously, the earth-filled flower-pot base of the shipping container can't be very large; otherwise, shipping charges would be ruinous. Now, a healthy bare-root rose bush shipped from the nursery where it was grown will have roots from eighteen inches to more than two feet long, and will require a planting hole about two feet in diameter if the roots are to be spread out as they should be. How much of this root system would remain if the bush had to be pruned to fit a six-inch flower pot? Obviously, very little.

In my experience, container-shipped roses are slow starters and don't catch up with bare-root plants till they have been grown in the ground a year.

The only advantage I can see for container-shipped bushes is that they can be planted late in the spring when the weather is too warm to permit the planting of bare-root roses. In this respect, they are a boon. But I can't see much use in buying them for early planting.

As for the locally potted roses, much depends upon the skill and understanding of the dealer. With moderate root pruning, a bare-root plant can be accommodated reasonably well in a one-gallon can, the size usually used. If the earth ball is kept intact, potted roses can be planted just about any time with a fair chance of success. But that is assuming that the dealer started off with good rose bushes in a healthy state (not roses that were desiccated and already half dead), that suitable soil had been used in the potting operation, and that the roots have been treated with respect.

If you order roses from one of the major rose nurseries, your chances of receiving high-quality plants are extremely good. After all, these firms look to receive future orders from you. Nearly all of the better nurseries unconditionally guarantee their plants to live and grow.

Which reminds me of a tale that I heard from the owner of one of the larger rose nurseries. The firm guaranteed its roses, merely stipulating that any unsatisfactory plants be returned to the company for replacement or refund, and it was company policy to burn or otherwise destroy returned plants. The company had a secretary, whom I shall call Miss Nellie, whose duty it was to deal with all customer complaints. She dearly loved roses and couldn't bear to destroy rose bushes. So she made it a habit to sneak the returned bushes home and give them away to people who might want them. The company knew of her actions but chose to say nothing. So, for some thirty years Miss Nellie gave away plants that had been returned as sick or dying, and nobody was particularly surprised when most of these much-abused plants grew and bloomed prettily all over town.

Sometimes it happens that bare-root roses are delayed in transit, or that the box has stood for hours in hot sunshine on some station platform. In such circumstances the roses may suffer; long shoots may already have developed by the time the bushes are received, or the canes may look parched and wrinkled. If this should happen, it will usually suffice to soak the plants for two days in a bucket placed in a shady spot, making sure the roots are submerged up to the bud union. I find it also helps to add a little plant food to the water in the bucket: about a tablespoon of Ra-Pid-Gro, Ortho Liquid Plant Food, or Hyponex should do the trick. Further care should be taken to mound loose soil up over the canes when the bushes are planted, so that only an inch or so of the tops is showing, and to remove the soil very gradually over a three-week period.

If you are buying bare-root plants from a nursery, you have to rely on the company to pick out good, healthy bushes for you. You have a different problem when you are picking out your own from a display of packaged roses.

First, assuming that they have the varieties you want, look at the color of the canes. Healthy rose plants have either bright green or reddish canes; they don't have dead-leaf brown canes. Healthy rose plants look plump and juicy, not skinny and dried out. The canes should look smooth, not wrinkled. They should not be broken, and should have been pruned with a clean cut, not a ragged one. The eyes on the canes should be discernible as slightly swollen, reddish bumps, but preferably should not have grown into actual shoots. Under no circumstances should the bushes be in leaf.

Second, check the number and diameter of the canes. There should be three, preferably four canes, and they should be at least the diameter of your little finger. I don't think it is important how long the canes are, so long as each cane has four or more eyes.

In buying container-shipped or locally potted rose bushes, check the appearance of the canes; refuse any that look withered, discolored, or wrinkled. Don't accept plants having only one or two canes, or any with thin, spindly canes. Leaves on *potted* roses should cause no worry, since presumably the plants have their roots in nourishing soil. But given a choice between two other-wise equal bushes, one without buds and one in flower, take the first. The bush will suffer less shock in moving if it isn't in flower, and it won't have used up any energy in making flowers.

Every fall and spring, the gardening pages of the Sunday papers and the back pages of various gardening magazines are filled with advertisements for "bargain" roses. Some of them are mighty tempting to the beginner. There are those that offer rose bushes at ridiculously low prices: "One Dozen Everblooming Rose Bushes of Famous Varieties for Only $2.98, Postpaid. Satisfaction Guaranteed." And so on. Sometimes there will be a list of varieties offered; I can practically recite it from memory: Ami Quinard, Better Times, Christopher Stone, K. A. Victoria, Crimson Glory (maybe), Radiance, Golden Charm, Soeur Thérèse, Condesa de Sastago, Editor McFarland, Red Radiance, Picture. Occasionally, one will also find The Doctor, Briarcliff, Frau Karl Druschki, and Peace offered.

My observation is that most of these advertisements are misleading or downright dishonest. For one thing, most of the plants so sold are extremely small, often No. 2 size, and—assuming they survive—may take two or more years of careful tending to amount to anything. Furthermore, while it is true that many of the varieties advertised *are* famous, their fame is largely historic. Few of them will come up to the beauty or performance of the better new roses. It is like advertising a special on 1927 electric refrigerators. Finally, many of the nurseries that make these offers are unconcerned about accurate labeling. I have seen plants labeled Peace that turned out to be McGredy's Sunset or Condesa de Sas-

94

tago; and while both are good roses, neither can be compared to Peace.

One should be particularly careful about the claims of some nurseries concerning "miracle" roses: climbers said to cover the entire side of a two-story house in a single season; hybrid teas supposedly proof against severe low temperatures; roses advertised as immune to black spot. Such claims are at worst deliberate lies, at best serious exaggerations.

Of one thing you can be quite sure: when a genuine "miracle" rose does come along, it will be introduced by one of the large nurseries in this country, not by some firm you never heard of. The rose industry is too competitive, too wide awake, for any miraculous developments to escape the attention of the giants in the industry. It is a simple matter of dollars and cents. The potential for profit of a true miracle rose is so great that only the really big concerns have enough money and resources to be able to bid for it.

VII

Using Roses

A FEW years ago, one of the major rose nurseries, wishing to dramatize the multiplicity of uses to which roses can be put, landscaped an entire suburban home with nothing but roses. Enthusiastic as I am about roses, I don't think I would wish to limit myself wholly to them; it would mean depriving myself of too many other charming flowers. And there are other considerations, some practical and some aesthetic.

From a practical standpoint, I must object to the amount of spraying that would be entailed if the whole of our property were landscaped with roses. Granted, there are a few shrub roses that are virtually immune to black spot, but they represent only a small proportion of rosedom; most roses need regular chemical protection against fungus diseases, not to mention insects, many of which regard the rose as highly edible. (See Chapter X.)

96

From the aesthetic standpoint, I am afraid that a property decorated wholly with roses would not display them to best advantage. Jewelers show diamonds on a piece of black velvet. Any really feminine woman knows that her beauty appears to best advantage when she is in the company of a ruggedly masculine and not too handsome man. So it is with roses; their particular charm is best displayed against a simple background, and when many roses are used together, one must be careful lest, through exposure to too much beauty, the eye of the beholder become surfeited.

Let me pursue this question a little further. In Clarksville, Tennessee there is a house that was built on a lot that slopes up very sharply from the street. The architect took advantage of the ground contour, setting the house high and putting the garage in the basement. The driveway and turning circle at one side of the house, giving access to the garage, are a good ten feet below the level of the rest of the yard. At the back of the turning circle, the architect employed a high retaining wall, perhaps thirty feet long and about ten feet tall. This wall, which faces the street, could be something of an eyesore. However, half a dozen bushes of the old climber, Paul's Scarlet, are planted at the top of the wall, without support. Instead of climbing, they spill over the edge of the void, and in June, when this rose blooms, there is no prettier sight in town. The only drawback is that the owners of the house didn't select everblooming climbers that would stay in flower all summer.

What I'm trying to point out is that the peculiar effectiveness of this planting depends heavily upon the simple, dramatic way in which the plants are displayed.

There are many ways in which roses can be used.

97

I propose to discuss them under the following headings: in beds, in containers, on supports, as shrubs and hedges, and as ground covers.

Roses in Beds

I'm sure that the commonest way to grow roses is in beds. Not all rose beds, however, are effective. Some are too narrow, permitting only a single row of roses; the effect is skimpy and disappointing. Some are too wide, making it impossible to inspect and enjoy many of the specimens nearby, and posing many serious problems of weeding and tending. Some are too fussy—a mess of half round and triangular plantings interspersed with paths and birdbaths and gimcrackery, after the example of Victorian gardens. And some have too many different varieties planted in them.

The location of a rose bed must be determined by the direction of the sun, by the available space, and by the location of trees, walks, shrubs, building, retaining wall, fences, and similar factors. And in deciding on what shape to make a rose bed, I think the first and most basic consideration is the question of artistic suitability. The bed should have some logical, linear relationship to the rest of the property. It should not be merely capricious or whimsical. It may follow the line of a curved walk or driveway, in which case the bed will be curved. It may occupy a corner of a yard, in which case it might logically be triangular or L-shaped, or perhaps have a modified L-shape with the back edges following the right angle of the property lines and the front edge a flowing, free-form curve. It may be a simple rectangle, placed in relation to other rectangular flower beds and separated from them by a walk or a strip of lawn. But it should not be shaped like a circle, a crescent, or a star. Let's keep it suitable and logical.

I mentioned that a rose bed should not contain too many varieties. This may sound illogical, but there are many practical reasons for it. First, there is the question of color harmony and color contrast. The more varieties you have, the more difficult it becomes to work the differing shades into a harmonious, overall effect. Similarly, when you have a large number of different colors represented in a bed, it becomes all but impossible to achieve dramatic effects of contrast.

I fully understand the temptation to buy a great many different varieties of roses. You go through a nursery catalogue and you feel like a child with a dime to spend and a whole penny candy counter from which to choose. And so you end up buying one each of twelve or eighteen or twenty-four varieties. It is not till you begin trying to reconcile all the colors, not to mention the differing heights of varieties, that you realize what a problem you have created. The worst of it is that you don't find out you're in trouble till the roses are in bloom and it's too late to make changes that season. You will also be saddened by the spotty effect of the bloom: roses of different varieties tend to bloom and rest on different schedules.

I mentioned earlier that I acted for several years as rosarian for a municipal rose garden. This job involved not only supervising the planting and care of the garden, but its design, including the selection of varieties.

Now it is obvious that there is a difference between planting a home rose garden and a city rose garden. The home garden may have from a dozen to perhaps fifty plants; our municipal garden had about seven hundred. The home garden may have four or five beds at most; our municipal garden had twenty-nine. Obviously, it is easier to achieve broad effects of color harmony and color contrast in the municipal garden than in the average home garden. However, the general principles will be the same in both cases.

In planning the municipal garden, I used a module of six bushes of a single variety; that is, the number of roses of a single variety in any bed was always a multiple of six: six, twelve, or twenty-four, to be precise. The beds were designed to hold twenty-four bushes each. Thus, a bed might contain four varieties planted in blocks of six each; two varieties in plantings of twelve each; or might be devoted to twenty-four bushes of a single variety. In practice, this system worked out extremely well. Color harmonies were easily achieved: for instance, a bed containing four blocks of roses, starting at one end with six pale pinks, then six deep pinks, then six more deep pinks, and finally six pale pinks. Strong contrasts were also possible: for example, in the front of a bed a dozen white floribundas, and behind them a row of a dozen deep red floribundas.

For home-garden layouts, I would recommend a module of two or three, preferably the latter. Again, there are practical reasons for using three of a variety, the principal one being cost. Most of the major rose nurseries offer their roses at a reduced price when three or more of a variety are purchased at one time. For example, the Fall 1973 Conard-Pyle Company catalogue quotes the following prices on the rose Granada: "$3.95 each— 3 or more, $3.60 each." In the Jackson & Perkins catalogue, I find the following pricing for King's Ransom: "$3.95 each; 3 for $10.95."

As you can see, there is no advantage in buying two roses of one variety, but a considerable savings in lots of three.

Aside from the price advantage, a module of three works out nicely from an aesthetic standpoint. Three rose bushes of the same variety planted together make a great deal of show, particularly if they are set out in a triangle so that the tops can come together in a large mass. As we shall see in the plans, this arrangement is easily accomplished in a bed having two rows of plants.

The dimensions of a rose bed must be predicated upon the space requirements of the various roses to be planted in it. Miniature roses can be planted nine inches to a foot apart. A few dwarf floribundas can be set from a foot to eighteen inches apart. Nearly all other bedding roses—hybrid teas, grandifloras, many hybrid perpetuals, and nearly all floribundas—should be spaced from twenty-four to thirty inches apart, except in California, Florida, and one or two other very-mild-climate areas where rose bushes grow to exceptional size. In such areas, the planting distance may vary from thirty-six to forty-eight inches. In most parts of the country, a rose bed having an area of one hundred square feet will comfortably accommodate twenty-four bushes.

By way of illustrating the almost endless possibilities of rose-bed design, I show in Figure 1 three different arrangements of a bed measuring four feet by twenty-five feet and containing one hundred square feet of space. You will notice that the roses are planted in two straight rows, but that the plants are staggered between the front and back row. Roses in the front row are twenty-four

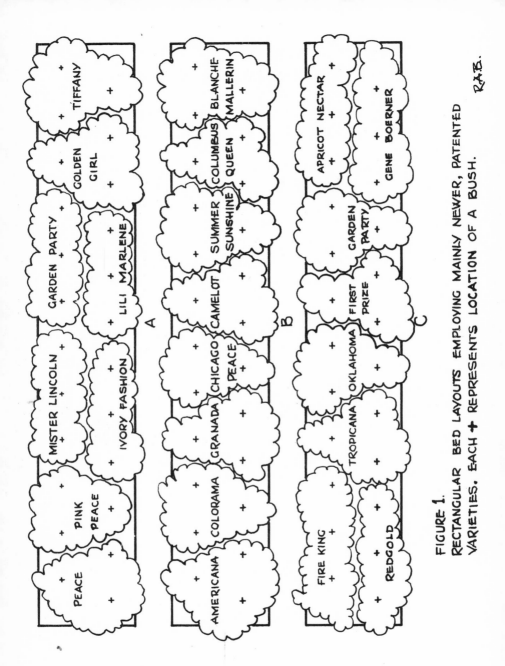

FIGURE 1.
RECTANGULAR BED LAYOUTS EMPLOYING MAINLY NEWER, PATENTED
VARIETIES. EACH + REPRESENTS LOCATION OF A BUSH.

R.A.B.

inches apart, as are those in the back row, but because of the staggered arrangement, the diagonal spacing is twenty-seven inches, allowing for a little better circulation of air and more elbow room. I show the front row of bushes set in one foot from the front of the bed, and the back row one foot from the rear of the bed. (Of course if a wider spacing were used, fewer bushes could be accommodated.)

Bed A is designed for a mixture of hybrid teas and floribundas. This bed is intended to give a very strong and dramatic color contrast when it is in bloom. In the center of the bed I show Ivory Fashion, a creamy white floribunda, in front of Mister Lincoln, a tall, deep crimson hybrid tea. Reversing the color contrast, I have Lili Marlene, a crimson floribunda, in front of Garden Party, a tall, near-white hybrid tea. That is enough strong contrast for one bed. Consequently, I use a clump of roses having a good transitional color on each side of this dramatic center area: on the left I have set Pink Peace, a vibrant medium pink rose; and on the right, Golden Girl, a clear yellow. On the extreme left I have Peace, a delicate blend of ivory, gold, and pink, which will harmonize pleasantly with the tones of Pink Peace. Tiffany, on the extreme right, is a blend of pink and gold; the latter tone will pick up and repeat the yellow of Golden Girl.

Bed B is wholly different in conception. It is designed to hold nothing but hybrid teas, and it is based on the principle of color gradations: that is, progression rather than contrast. It starts off on the left with Americana, a brilliant and unusually vibrant crimson. Next is Colorama, a bicolor in gold and either Chinese red or deep watermelon pink, depending on the season. Granada is an unbelievably brilliant blend of scarlet, cherry, and gold. Chicago Peace repeats the cherry and gold of Granada, but adds pale pink and ivory tones. Camelot is a coral pink, bordering on salmon-orange tones. Summer Sunshine is a clear, golden yellow, which should pick up the faint yellow or orange cast of Camelot. Columbus Queen is a clear orchid pink, with a darker orchid tone to the reverse of the petals. And Blanche Mallerin is as white as a rose can be. As you can see, this bed runs a scale or gamut from deep red to white. I have carefully avoided the inclusion of any roses in this bed that show any tendency toward lavender or old rose tones, which would swear horribly at the other colors.

Bed C allows for both color contrast and tonal harmonies. Its conception is a bit daring, but I believe it would be effective. At the left is a clump of the floribunda Fire King, which is a solid, brilliant vermilion. Contrasting with it is the clump of Red Gold, a brilliant new floribunda in gay tones of yellow and cherry red. At the extreme right of the bed are two more clumps of floribundas of contrasting colors: Apricot Nectar in the rear is a blend of apricot and pink, while Gene Boerner, in the front, is a clear, clean pink. The whole center of the bed is devoted to hybrid teas. The first of the hybrid teas on the left, Tropicana, is a clear tangerine color, which should provide a transition from the vermilion tones of the floribundas to the almost crimson-black color of Oklahoma. First Prize shifts back to lighter tones: it is a rich pink suffused with dark pink. Garden Party, the last of the hybrid teas, is an almost white rose, the edges of the petals faintly tinged with shell pink; it should provide a good transition to the pink tones in both Apricot Nectar and Gene Boerner.

You are probably wondering what these beds would cost. I have checked their prices in the 1973 catalogues of four major mail-order rose nurseries, which among them handle all of the varieties mentioned: Conard-Pyle, Armstrong, Jackson & Perkins, and Melvin Wyant. On this basis, the roses in Bed A would cost $70.05; those in Bed B, $75.80; and those in Bed C, $82.50.

The roses selected in Figure 1 are almost all relatively new, patented varieties, and as such they are quite expensive. To show that the same principles can be applied to less expensive rose varieties, in Figure 2 I give three possible layouts, based largely on the use of older, patent-expired roses, many of which are in all ways comparable to the finest of the new roses.

The reader should, however, remember that in addition to the cost of the roses one must figure on other costs, such as for edging, peat moss, bone meal, and so on.

In Bed D, a strong contrast is developed in the center of the planting for dramatic effect. The deep red floribunda Garnette is placed in front of the ivory, pink, and gold of Peace. The strong pink of China Doll should contrast sharply with the clear yellow of Eclipse behind it. Charlotte Armstrong, a light red or very deep pink hybrid tea, provides a good transition to the deep red of Crimson Glory on the extreme left. To the right of center, Blanche Mallerin, one of the whitest of roses, provides a transition to the deep crimson of Mirandy on the extreme right. The two crimson masses on each end give the bed symmetry and balance. A contrast of heights is provided in the center, since both Garnette and China Doll are quite low growing, while Peace and Eclipse are both tall varieties.

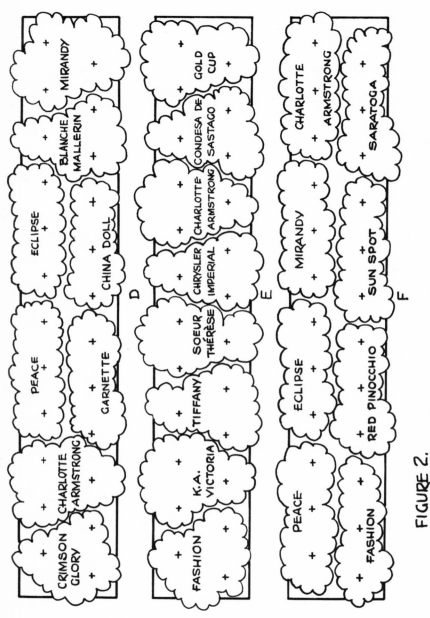

FIGURE 2.
RECTANGULAR BED LAYOUTS EMPLOYING MAINLY OLDER, PATENT-
EXPIRED VARIETIES. EACH + REPRESENTS LOCATION OF A BUSH.

R.A.B.

Bed E offers a series of pleasant color transitions as well as a certain amount of contrast in height. The two ends of the bed contain relatively low-growing floribundas; the rest of the bed is devoted to rather tall-growing hybrid teas. Fashion, on the left, is a soft peachy pink suffused with gold, while K. A. Victoria is a crisp white; Tiffany is pink and gold, and Soeur Thérèse is a bright, clear yellow. Chrysler Imperial is a deep red, rather like Crimson Glory. Charlotte Armstrong is a light red or deep pink, depending upon how your mind works. Condesa de Sastago is watermelon pink and gold, while Gold Cup is a deep, pure gold. You will notice that this arrangement allows for strong contrasts of color without tonal conflicts.

Bed F is a departure from all the other layouts. The entire front row is devoted to floribundas: Fashion, peach pink with gold shading; Red Pinocchio, a solid carmine red; Sun Spot, a clear, sunny yellow; and Saratoga, an exceptionally clean white. The back row is all hybrid teas, selected to contrast dramatically with the floribundas in front of them: Peace, an ivory, pink, and gold blend; Eclipse, bright yellow; Mirandy, crimson; and Charlotte Armstrong, light red or deep pink.

I would not have hesitated to use any of the layouts shown in Figure 2 in the Municipal Rose Garden, for the roses are of the highest quality. At current 1973 prices, Bed D would cost $76.20; Bed E, $62.15; and Bed F, $73.50.

Rose lovers put a premium upon novelty and seek it avidly. In recent years the big novelty has been lavender roses. Mankind has a short memory and a fickle heart. When hybrid teas were very new, breeders sought to produce "clean" colors—pure yellows, pure whites, clear pinks and reds without any trace of blue in them. The color that we now designate "old rose," which has a definite lavender cast, was the typical color of pink roses a century ago. Many of the deep reds had a purple tinge, and as the blossoms of both pink and red roses faded, many of them took on a pronounced bluish tinge. To nineteenth-century rosarians, this fault, known as "blueing," was regarded as most undesirable, particularly in show roses.

At the same time that hybridists were trying to get the bluish tinge out of the pinks and reds, they were trying to get the pinks and reds out of the blue—to isolate the blue coloration in its true form. While most modern hybridists believe, on the basis of genetic study and examination of the pigmentation in roses, that a true blue rose is a natural impossibility, the search for one has gone on for a long time and still continues. A rose called Veilchenblau (Blue Violet), a rather ugly purple rambler, made something of a splash when it was introduced from Germany in 1909. Happily, it had a very brief vogue, although plants of it are still to be seen in many places today. As I pointed out in Chapter II, many of the gallicas show a lavender or purplish coloration, some markedly so, such as Charles de Mills, Rose du Maître d'Ecole, Président de Sèze, and Cardinal de Richelieu; the last mentioned is very nearly blue. Some of the hybrid perpetuals also display this bluish cast, particularly Reine des Violettes. So there is nothing particularly new about lavender coloration in roses.

Nevertheless, the present generation of hybridists are exerting themselves to produce violet garden roses of high quality, and we now have a fair selection from which to choose. I suspect that the rose that was primarily responsible for the revival of interest in lavender coloration was Sterling Silver, which was introduced in 1957. It is a pale, silvery lavender, almost a gray. It has an intense perfume, as is common to most of the lavender roses, and its form is exquisite. Ladies interested in flower arranging became quite hysterical over Sterling Silver when Jackson & Perkins brought it out. Immediately, other major rose nurseries appeared with lavender roses, some of which were hybrid teas, and some floribundas.

I wish I liked them better. However, there are many who consider the new lavender roses exquisite, and for their benefit I am including a couple of bed layouts featuring these roses.

My observation has been that lavender roses clash badly—almost disastrously—with most other rose colors. I do not advise planting them in any bed containing pinks or reds, or blends of pink or red. They are handsome, however, when grown in isolation, or when paired with white or clear yellow roses. Figure 3 shows two possible layouts. The beds are twelve and one-half feet long by four feet wide, containing fifty square feet of space, and will each accommodate a dozen rose bushes on a twenty-four-inch spacing.

Bed G contains two clumps of tall, pale lavender hybrid teas: Sterling Silver and Song of Paris. These occupy the rear center position in the bed, and are flanked on both sides by the clear yellow Golden Girl. The front of the bed contains two clumps of a really splendid floribunda, Angel Face, which is a dark violet, so placed as to contrast with Golden Girl and to be made more dramatic by the presence of the white floribunda Sara-

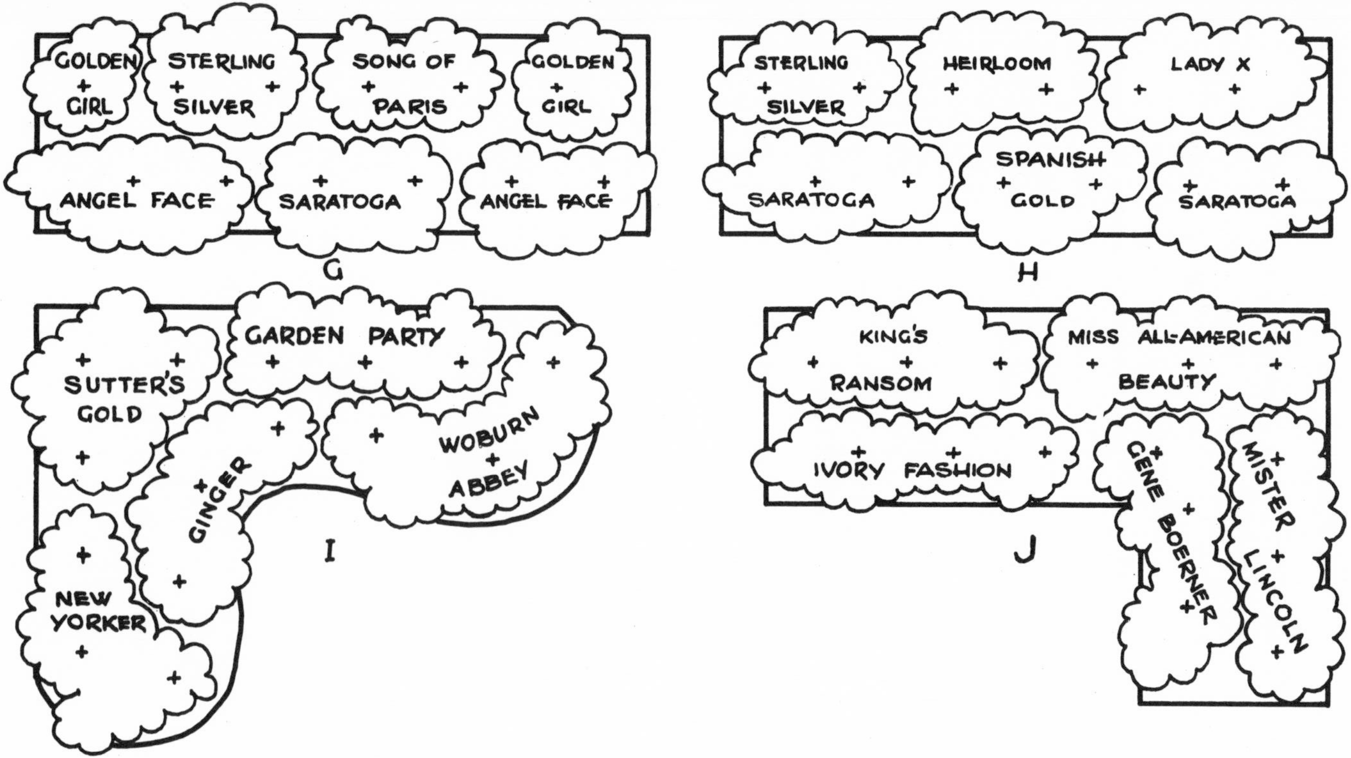

FIGURE 3.

TWO SMALL RECTANGULAR BED LAYOUTS – G AND H – FEATURING LAVENDER ROSES, AND TWO FENCE-CORNER GROUPINGS. EACH + REPRESENTS LOCATION OF A BUSH.

G

GOLDEN GIRL | STERLING SILVER | SONG OF PARIS | GOLDEN GIRL
ANGEL FACE | SARATOGA | ANGEL FACE

H

STERLING SILVER | HEIRLOOM | LADY X
SARATOGA | SPANISH GOLD | SARATOGA

J

MISS ALL-AMERICAN BEAUTY | MISTER LINCOLN
GENE BOERNER
KING'S RANSOM | IVORY FASHION

I

SUTTER'S GOLD | GARDEN PARTY | WOBURN ABBEY
GINGER
NEW YORKER

RAB.

toga. I know this bed would be very distinctive, and I think it would be quaint and pleasing.

Bed H uses lavender roses only in the back row: the two clumps of pale lavender Sterling Silver and Lady X, on the extreme left and right respectively, are intended to add to the dramatic quality of the very dark lavender hybrid tea Heirloom in the center. The front of the bed puts the white floribunda Saratoga on either side of the bright yellow floribunda Spanish Gold. This, too, should be a pleasing and distinctive planting.

One thing I must say about lavender roses: they all smell lovely.

Being half to three-quarters as large as those shown in Figures 1 and 2, the beds in Figure 3 will cost considerably less. At current 1973 prices, the cost of the roses works out as follows: Bed G, $30.50; Bed H, $46.90; Bed I, $46.15; and Bed J, $50.85.

Beds G and H have already been discussed; it remains to describe I and J, which are very different.

Sometimes a small rose bed, if it is strategically placed where it catches and holds the eye, can be showier than a much larger bed less dramatically situated. The two L-shaped beds shown in Figure 3 illustrate this principle. Such a bed can be established in a fence corner, in the angle formed by two house walls, or at the intersection of two walks. The long leg of each bed is twelve and one-half feet, the short leg is ten feet, both being measured along the back, and the width is four feet. Each will hold fifteen rose bushes.

Bed I, which has a free-form front edge, is quite brazen and daring in its color combinations, and should be a traffic stopper. It employs three different and very showy hybrid tea varieties: New Yorker, deep crimson;

Sutter's Gold, yellow suffused with cherry; and Garden Party, white tinged pink. All three bloom very profusely. In front of these are placed two really startling floribundas: Ginger, a vermilion-orange, and Woburn Abbey, a blend of vermilion and gold.

Bed J is more restrained. The background consists of three outstanding varieties of hybrid teas: King's Ransom, an unusually large yellow rose; Miss All-American Beauty, a clean, medium pink rose of unusual clarity of color; and Mister Lincoln, a deep crimson of immense size. The front of the bed contains three plants each of Ivory Fashion, a creamy white floribunda, and Gene Boerner, an exquisite light pink floribunda.

I have gone into some detail and shown ten different bed layouts because I wished to emphasize that designing an effective rose bed is more than a matter of digging some holes and sticking in some rose bushes. Insofar as my experience and aesthetic understandings allow, I try to follow certain principles, which I have had to formulate for myself, for I have yet to see them expressed or discussed in the literature on rose culture. Perhaps it will help if I summarize the more important principles.

1. Effectiveness is increased by planting several bushes of the same variety together: at least two, preferably three.

2. There should be some logic in the progression of color through a bed; variations on this principle are almost endless, like variations on a musical theme.

3. Use solid-colored roses as foils—an idea that needs some explaining. Suppose that you have three each of three blends, roses that are a mixture of several delicate colors. For the sake of illustration, let us suppose that they are Peace, Medallion, and American Heritage. If

TROPICANA
PP1969 © *Jackson & Perkins Co.*

PINK PEACE
PP1759 © *The Conard Pyle Co.*

CHICAGO PEACE
PP2037 © *The Conard Pyle Co.*

FIRST PRIZE

PP2774 © *Jackson & Perkins Co.*

MEDALLION

PP2997 © *Jackson & Perkins Co.*

COLORAMA
PP2862 © The Conard Pyle Co.

PASCALI
PP2592 © Armstrong Nurseries Inc.

GARDEN PARTY
*PP1814 © Armstrong
Nurseries Inc.*

APOLLO
PP3322 © *Armstrong Nurseries Inc.*

FLORIBUNDAS

RED GOLD
PP3006 © *Jackson & Perkins Co.*

SPANISH SUN
PP2809 © *Jackson & Perkins Co.*

EUROPEANA
PP2540 © *The Conard Pyle Co.*

GENE BOERNER
PP2885   © Jackson & Perkins Co.

APERITIF
© Jackson & Perkins Co.

ANGEL FACE
PP2792   © The Conard Pyle Co.

BAHIA
PPAF   © Armstrong Nurseries Inc.

SPARTAN
Pat. Exp. © *Jackson & Perkins Co.*

APRICOT NECTAR
PP2594 © *Jackson & Perkins Co.*

FIRE KING
PP1758 © *The Conard Pyle Co.*

CIRCUS PARADE
PP2150 © *Armstrong*
Nurseries Inc.
(sport of Circus)

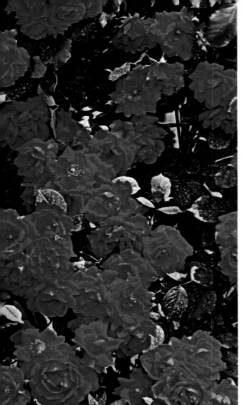

BLAZE
Pat. Exp. © *Jackson & Perkins Co.*

RHONDA
PP2854 © *The Conard Pyle Co.*

ROYAL GOLD
PP1849 © *Jackson & Perkins Co.*

DON JUAN
PP1864 © *Jackson & Perkins Co.*

MINIATURES

SCARLET GEM
PP2155   © The Conard Pyle Co.

SHOOTING STAR
© The Conard Pyle Co.

BABY GOLD STAR
© The Conard Pyle Co.

RED IMP
© The Conard Pyle Co.

these blends are planted adjacent to one another, the particular delicacy of coloration will be largely lost. Separate them with clear, solid-colored roses such as Pink Peace or Royal Highness, dark and light pink respectively; or Chrysler Imperial or Mister Lincoln, crimson; or Eclipse or King's Ransom, clear yellow; or Blanche Mallerin or Pascali, pure white. Following this same principle, avoid planting several slightly different pink varieties together. Instead, use divergent colors as foils to emphasize their individual differences.

4. Deliberately juxtapose roses of strongly contrasting or complementary colors for dramatic effect, such as white Saratoga in front of almost black Oklahoma. The eye will be drawn immediately by this powerful contrast. This same effect can be used to give a planting balance: the focal point of strong color contrast can be placed in the center of the bed, for example; or two focal points can be established, one at either end.

5. Consider the vertical aspect of your layout. Don't put tall varieties in front of short ones, and avoid the sawtooth effect created by alternating tall and short varieties. If you have pronouncedly low-growing roses, use them at the ends or in the front row, and put your tall ones in the center and rear.

Growing Roses in Containers

There are several situations in which it might be desirable to grow roses in some sort of container rather than planting them in the open ground. Apartment dwellers in cities may have no better place to grow flowers than on a balcony or a roof. For them, container gardening is a necessity. A paved patio may need dressing up with flowering plants; again, containers may be the best answer, both from a practical and an aesthetic standpoint. Finally, there are those persons who live in extremely cold regions—Alaska, for example—who may wish to grow roses but have experienced disappointments when the bushes could not endure the extreme cold of winter. Again, containers that can be brought into shelter during the winter and set outdoors during the mild season may provide the only possible answer.

Roses can be grown successfully in suitable containers. The ubiquitous redwood planter tub, if it is sufficiently large, will serve the purpose very well. However, to properly house a hybrid tea or floribunda, other than a dwarf variety, will require a planter whose diameter is at least twenty-four inches, and these things are terribly costly.

I have given much thought to the problem of suitable rose containers, and believe that the planter shown in Figure 4 represents a highly practical solution. The sides, ends, and bottom are made of waterproof exterior plywood three-fourths of an inch thick. Redwood is used only sparingly as supports for the bottom. The support battens are one and a quarter inches wide and three-fourths of an inch thick; any lumber mill can rip them from a redwood board. (Incidentally, if redwood is hard to come by in your area, you can safely substitute pine or fir that has been pressure-impregnated against termites.)

While there is undoubtedly some difference in lumber prices in different parts of the country, I would estimate that these planters, as shown, can be built for less than eight dollars apiece. You can get the sides, ends, and bot-

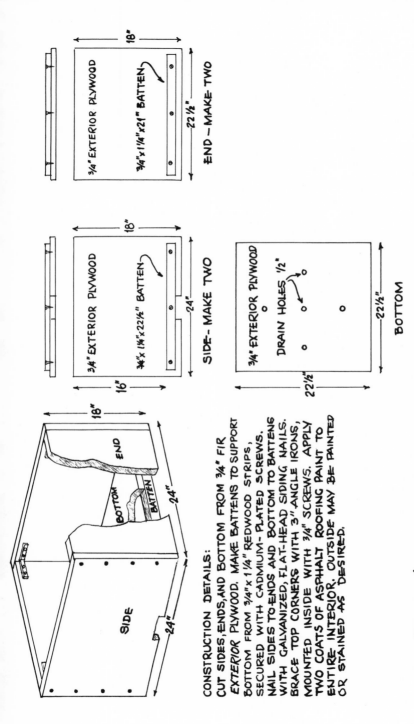

END — MAKE TWO

3/4" EXTERIOR PLYWOOD

3/4" x 1 1/4" x 21" BATTEN

18"

22 1/2"

SIDE — MAKE TWO

3/4" EXTERIOR PLYWOOD

3/4" x 1 1/4" x 22 1/2" BATTEN

18"

24"

16"

BOTTOM

3/4" EXTERIOR PLYWOOD

DRAIN HOLES 1/2"

22 1/2"

22 1/2"

SIDE

END

BOTTOM

BATTEN

18"

24"

24"

CONSTRUCTION DETAILS:

CUT SIDES, ENDS, AND BOTTOM FROM 3/4" FIR EXTERIOR PLYWOOD. MAKE BATTENS TO SUPPORT BOTTOM FROM 3/4" x 1 1/4" REDWOOD STRIPS, SECURED WITH CADMIUM-PLATED SCREWS. NAIL SIDES TO ENDS AND BOTTOM TO BATTENS WITH GALVANIZED, FLAT-HEAD SIDING NAILS. BRACE TOP CORNERS WITH 3" ANGLE IRONS, MOUNTED INSIDE WITH 3/4" SCREWS. APPLY TWO COATS OF ASPHALT ROOFING PAINT TO ENTIRE INTERIOR. OUTSIDE MAY BE PAINTED OR STAINED AS DESIRED.

FIGURE 4.
PLYWOOD CONTAINER FOR ROSES

R.A.B.

toms for two of these containers out of a single sheet of exterior plywood measuring four by eight feet. The rest of the materials will cost very little. To assure a good fit, unless you have a well-equipped woodworking shop at your disposal, you will do well to have the plywood parts cut to dimension at the lumberyard. Plywood this heavy is awkward to cut from the sheet, but a lumberyard can saw the parts to size in a jiffy.

I suspect that most people would want containers of the size shown, particularly if they have to be moved into shelter during the winter. Earth is heavy, and even one of these two-foot-square boxes will weigh quite a lot. However, the container shown is designed to hold a single, specimen hybrid tea or large floribunda. A box twice as long, two feet by four feet, will hold two bushes comfortably, and one might even crowd three into it, although regular pruning would be required to keep the bushes within bounds. For that matter, the length could be increased to six or eight feet, by a simple extension of the basic plan. In reasonably temperate areas, where special winter protection of the plants would not be necessary and the boxes could stay outdoors the year round, the longer boxes, six or eight feet, would be very effective, as they could be planted and treated much as one would handle an ordinary bed. One might, for example, use several long containers to form a wall around the outer edge of a patio. Or one of the small boxes shown might be placed on either side of the front entrance to the house; planted with a vigorous, really everblooming floribunda like Ginger or Red Gold, for example, they would be extremely decorative.

Even the small two-foot-square container could accommodate three—maybe four—floribundas if care were taken to select the lower-growing varieties. Possible selections might include Bon Bon, Europeana, Chatter, Spanish Sun, China Doll, Angel Face, and if you can still find them on the market, Pigmy Red, Pigmy Gold, and Golden Garnette. Care should be taken, however, to increase the frequency of spraying, as the poor air circulation that results from crowding is an invitation to fungus infections.

Miniature roses, of course, are naturally well suited to container growing. The basic container shown would accommodate as many as a dozen miniatures without excessive crowding. However, the depth of the container should be reduced to twelve inches, which should be more than sufficient.

Miniature roses can be grown successfully in ordinary commercial window boxes secured outside the house, in flower pots, or in strawberry jars. Actually, I think the last is the most attractive way of growing them. One can also improvise a container that gives much the same effect as a strawberry jar. The only catch is that you have to lay hands on an old-fashioned wooden nail keg. Nowadays, nails usually come in boxes. However, if you can find a nail keg, drill several half-inch holes in the bottom to assure drainage, and make a number of circular openings in the sides, at different levels, with a two-inch expansion bit mounted in a carpenter's brace. Give the inside of the keg a couple of heavy coats of asphalt roof paint, and when it is dry, fill it with earth. Not only can you plant the whole top area with miniature roses, but you can also plant them in the holes in the sides. You can stain or paint the outside of the keg, or leave it unfinished and let the wood weather.

In planting any of the containers described, put about

one and a half inches of coarse gravel in the bottom. On top of that, put a layer of wood charcoal, and then fill the box to the top with a growing medium consisting of one part of Canadian peat moss and two parts of good soil, thoroughly mixed together. I think it will materially improve plant performance if a little bone meal is added to the mixture; I would use one standard measuring cup of bone meal in the two-foot-square box, and proportionally more in the larger boxes.

Roses are greedy plants, requiring a lot of food and moisture. Regular watering is essential to container growing, since soil will dry out much faster in a container than it will in the ground. Regular feeding is also essential, as the roots are confined to the soil you provide. I would suggest monthly feeding of the plants in the container by dissolving one tablespoon of Ra-Pid-Gro or Ortho Liquid Plant Food in one gallon of water and using the mixture for watering when the soil in the container is fairly dry. Feeding should be initiated in early spring and continued until the beginning of fall weather, when it should be discontinued till the following spring.

Roses on Supports

While some pillar roses or moderate climbers will stand alone, most climbers and all ramblers need to be grown on something that will keep them off the ground.

There is no lack of suitable pillars and climbers; any rose nursery can supply more varieties than anyone could possibly use in a home garden. There is, however, a dearth of ready-made trellises and other supports for roses. The commonest commercially produced rose trellis is a miserable, flimsy affair consisting of a number of narrow wooden slats held together at the base and spread out at the top in the shape of a fan. It isn't worth owning. Neither are the metal trellises made on the same pattern.

The main trouble with these fan-shaped trellises, aside from the fact that the wooden ones have a nasty habit of rotting and breaking off at ground level, is that the top is not wide enough: the maximum that the canes can be trained to spread is around a 45-degree angle. When a climbing rose is grown so nearly vertical, it tends to flower only at the top. To make a climber really bloom heavily for nearly the entire length of the canes, train the canes as nearly horizontal as possible. I'm not sure what the mechanism is, whether it is exposure of the upper side of the cane to more sunlight, or simply the change in orientation of the cane; whatever the reason, when a cane is trained horizontally, it will begin pushing out a large number of side branches—"laterals"—which will point straight up, and virtually all of these laterals will flower.

If you want a good trellis, my advice is to build it yourself. In Figure 5, I show a modular trellis unit that is both easy and inexpensive to build. As you will notice, the height is six feet, exactly equal to the length of the two top horizontal members. Each unit calls for two eight-foot, four-by-four cedar or redwood fence posts, sunk two feet in the ground and set in concrete. The horizontal bars are merely lengths of one-half-inch steel rod, the kind used for reinforcing concrete, which any lumberyard can supply. It's not expensive and can be easily cut with a hacksaw. After the bars are cut to

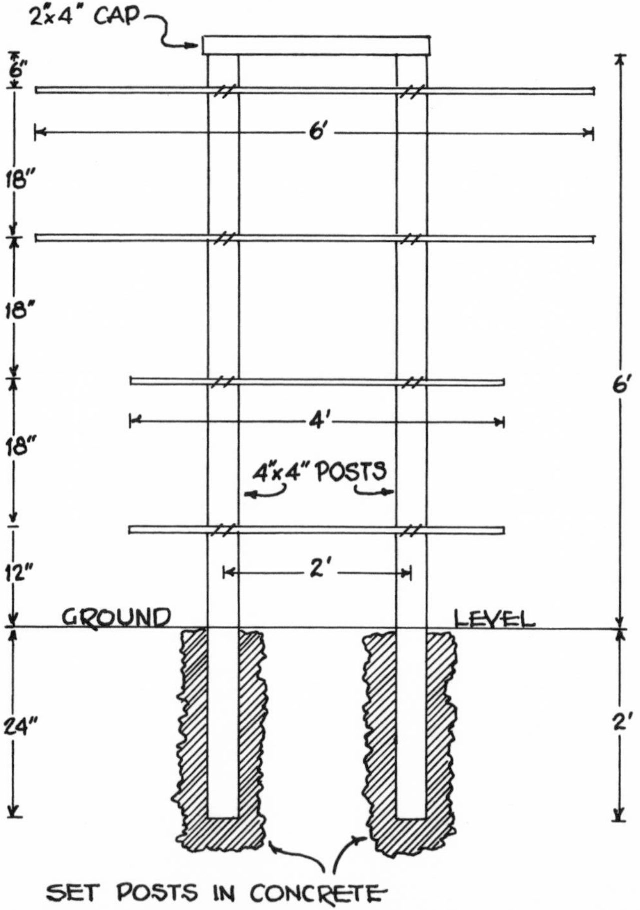

CONSTRUCTION DETAILS:

UPRIGHTS ARE 4"x4" FENCE POSTS, 8' LONG – CEDAR, REDWOOD, OR PINE PRESSURE-TREATED AGAINST ROT AND TERMITES. HORIZONTALS ARE ½" DIAMETER STEEL CONCRETE – REINFORCING RODS, SECURED TO POSTS WITH HEAVY STAPLES. UPRIGHTS SHOULD BE SET IN CONCRETE; JOIN THE TOPS OF THE POSTS WITH A 2"x 4" CAP. IF ROSES ARE TO BE PLANTED TO GROW ON FRONT AND BACK OF TRELLIS, INSTALL A SECOND SET OF HORIZONTALS ON BACK SIDE. A ROW OF THESE MODULES WITH UPPER RODS TOUCHING WILL FORM ANY DESIRED LENGTH OF TRELLIS. IF BUILT IN THIS WAY, TIE UNIT TOGETHER WITH CONTINUOUS 2"x4" CAP. PAINT THE ENTIRE STRUCTURE LIBERALLY.

FIGURE 5.

MODULAR TRELLIS UNIT FOR PILLAR OR CLIMBING ROSES.

R.A.B.

length, merely staple them to the face of the posts, using heavy fence staples. I should advise giving the bars a preliminary coat of rust-preventive paint, and then painting the whole trellis heavily with a good house paint.

One could, of course, use wooden bars in place of the steel ones, but they have an unhappy tendency to twist and bend under the considerable weight of a heavy climber. There is still another advantage in using steel reinforcing rods: they have little ring-shaped bumps about every six inches to facilitate their being tied together with wire when they are used in concrete work. These bumps help a lot in tying the rose canes to the rods.

You will notice that I show a length of two-by-four as a cap across the top of the two posts to render them secure and steady. If you elect to put up several of these modular units in a line to form a long trellis, set them six feet apart and use twelve-foot two-by-four caps to tie the whole row of units together.

The dimensions of these units have been carefully selected. Nearly all climbers can be set six feet apart, and a trellis made up of these units will automatically give you this spacing.

As a division between two properties, nothing is any prettier (or more appreciated by your next-door neighbor) than a low fence covered with rampant climbers. Figure 6 shows a simple fence-trellis made on the same principle as the modular trellis unit. You can, if you wish, put all the steel rods on one side of the posts, but the appearance will be improved by alternating sides, as shown in the drawing. These reinforcing rods come in very long pieces, so that two or more posts can be crossed with a single length of rod.

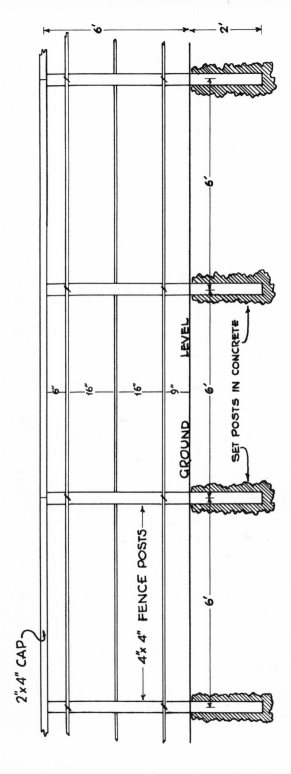

CONSTRUCTION DETAILS:

UPRIGHTS ARE 4"x4" FENCE POSTS, 6' LONG — CEDAR, REDWOOD, OR PINE PRESSURE TREATED AGAINST ROT AND TERMITES. HORIZONTALS ARE ½" STEEL CONCRETE - REINFORCING RODS SECURED TO POSTS WITH HEAVY STAPLES. SET POSTS IN CONCRETE AND CAP CONTINUOUSLY WITH 2"x4". PAINT STRUCTURE LIBERALLY.

FIGURE 6.

LOW MODULAR FENCE-TRELLIS FOR CLIMBERS OR RAMBLERS.

RAB

If I were to build a fence like this, I would plant a climber in front of each fence post, and then put one or two low-growing roses between the posts, set out about eighteen inches from the fence line. A good rose to plant between posts would be the old polyantha, The Fairy.

Virtually any fence can be used for training roses, provided it receives enough sunlight. A rail fence, or one of the post-and-plank fences such as are commonly used in Kentucky, Tennessee, and elsewhere to enclose exercise yards for horses, provides as good a support as one could ask for. Either of these fences consists mainly of horizontal structures to which canes can be tied in a horizontal position. Much less convenient to use are those types of fences in which most of the members run vertically, such as picket fences and the redwood privacy fences that one finds in so many suburban back yards. Lacking horizontal supports, these fences are awkward to use as rose trellises. Probably the best expedient is to install a number of screw eyes in the fence to which canes can be attached.

Here I find it necessary to digress for a moment. In northern Europe, one will frequently see trees and vines espaliered against masonry walls. Metal hooks are driven into the stone or brick and used to attach the stems and branches so that the plant grows flat against the wall. From an aesthetic standpoint, these espaliered things are handsome; pears, apples, peaches, grapes, and roses are frequently seen that have been handled in this way and that seem to do unusually well under these artificial conditions.

The reason that espaliering works so well in countries like England and Holland is that the average annual temperature is quite low—definitely chilly by our standards. An expanse of wall not only provides shelter against chilling winds, but it absorbs heat during the day from the sun and radiates it during the cool nights. If this technique is used in many warmer areas of the United States, however, there is a strong possibility of killing the plant. Summer temperatures in southerly parts of the United States are so high that the gardener's problem is how to keep plants cool, rather than how to keep them warm. A rose or other plant espaliered flat against an expanse of wall or solid board fence, such as a woven redwood privacy fence, is likely to die from too much heat and too little circulation of air. In cool, northern areas, however, the technique is employed with great success.

Figure 7 shows an adaptation of a special support of a type that, so far as I know, was developed in France; in any case, these devices are seen there in some of the French rose gardens to support very rampant climbers and ramblers. The technique employed is to train the rose canes spirally around the support. The horizontal rods, set at right angles to each other, permit the development of a sort of spreading tree form, which creates a three-dimensional effect, rather than the essentially two-dimensional effect produced by a rose trained against one side of a trellis. It is also possible to plant two climbers on opposite sides of this device and train them both in the same spiral form; if two varieties of contrasting colors are used, the effect obtained is novel and pleasing.

I have shown dimensions on this drawing, but they are purely suggestive. The height above ground might be from six to eight feet. The horizontal rods should be longest at the top and shortest at the bottom, to accommodate the spreading top of the bush.

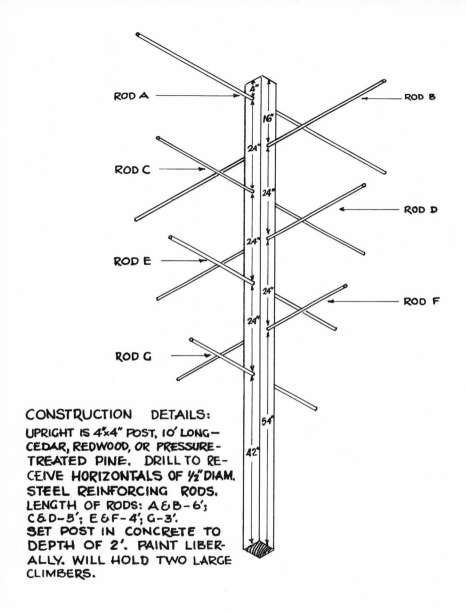

ROD A
ROD B
ROD C
ROD D
ROD E
ROD F
ROD G

4"
16"
24"
24"
24"
24"
24"
54"
42"

CONSTRUCTION DETAILS:
UPRIGHT IS 4"x4" POST, 10' LONG—
CEDAR, REDWOOD, OR PRESSURE-
TREATED PINE. DRILL TO RE-
CEIVE HORIZONTALS OF 1/2" DIAM.
STEEL REINFORCING RODS.
LENGTH OF RODS: A & B-6';
C & D-5'; E & F-4'; G-3'.
SET POST IN CONCRETE TO
DEPTH OF 2'. PAINT LIBER-
ALLY. WILL HOLD TWO LARGE
CLIMBERS.

FIGURE 7.
SPECIAL SUPPORT FOR RAMPANT CLIMBERS
RAB.

Whatever dimensions were used, I would make the post of four-by-four cedar or redwood and sink it solidly into the ground, preferably in concrete, to a depth of two feet or more. The bars, which should be steel reinforcing rods, are to be driven through holes drilled through the post. Obviously, if the rods are to be symmetrically arranged and the bars are to lie in a true horizontal position, the holes must be drilled with great exactitude. My advice is to have the lumberyard do them with a drill press, rather than trying to drill them yourself with a brace and bit.

Probably the most common causes of difficulty in training climbers on a trellis are impatience and the use of improper ties. A vertical-growing cane cannot be bent too quickly or too abruptly. Either you will break it or crush the wood fibers at the point where the principal bend occurs. However, with patience, a cane can be induced to grow horizontally by tying it in a gentle bend, waiting a week or so, and then making the bend a little sharper, until it is growing as you want it to. Obviously, only new, flexible canes can be induced to change their direction of growth. The bark is thin and easily bruised or abraded, so care should be exercised.

One of the worst mistakes you can make is to tie a cane with wire: not only will it cut into the bark, but it won't allow for the natural increase in the thickness of the cane as it matures, and the wire will often dig in and girdle it. Bark injuries almost always result in the development of stem canker, which starts much like an infection at the point of injury and soon spreads through the entire cane. Personally, I consider stem canker a much more serious disorder than black spot, as its symptoms are less readily noticeable.

In Europe many gardeners use flat strips of lead to fasten canes to trellis supports. These are about one-sixteenth of an inch thick and perhaps a quarter inch wide. One end is nailed to the trellis, and the other end is bent into a hook around the cane. The metal is stiff enough to hold the cane, but soft enough to yield as the cane grows, and the broad surface of the tie does not dig into the bark. I have seldom seen these ties used in this country, though I suppose one could have some specially made up. Most gardeners in this country use cloth strips to tie the canes; a strip of old nylon stocking is unsurpassed for this purpose, by the way. There is a right and a wrong way to make the tie, and I see the wrong one much more frequently than the right one. To do it wrong, simply pass a length of cloth strip around both the cane and the support in a single loop and tie a tight knot. This will strangle the cane just beautifully. The proper procedure is to pass the strip around the support and tie it tightly with a square knot, so that the strip is unlikely to slide back and forth on the support. Then take the two remaining ends of the strip and pass one over and one under the cane, form a *loose* loop, and tie the ends together in a second square knot.

Incidentally, many home owners, particularly those with small children or dogs, already have a splendid rose trellis without realizing it: a wire cyclone fence erected to keep the children or pets off the street. One could hardly design a more practical structure on which to grow climbing roses and other climbing plants: there are thousands of intersections in the wire mesh where a cane can be tied. As useful and necessary as these fences are, they are scarcely decorative in their natural, unadorned state. I don't know of anything that will improve the appearance of a cyclone fence more than planting climbers every six feet along its length and setting out hybrid teas or floribundas between the climbers.

Using Roses as Shrubs and Hedges

A number of the roses that are particularly well suited to grow as specimen shrubs or hedges have already been discussed in some detail in Chapter II. Most of the varieties used as shrubs are so employed because, for one reason or another, they are unsuited for use in beds but still have sufficient beauty to make them worth growing. Some have the fault of being too strong-growing: Mabelle Stearns and The Fairy, for example, take up too much space, growing only two or three feet tall but spreading to a diameter of five or six feet. Some are both too wide and too tall for small gardens, making what might be described as a small tree rather than a bush of manageable size: for example, most of the hybrid rugosas and hybrid musks and several of Wilhelm Kordes's roses such as Elmshorn, Sparrieshoop, and Kassel. Others are not only too large in stature for use in beds, but have the fault of blooming only once a year: for instance, Father Hugo's Rose and the little centifolia Petite de Hollande. Yet they make such a lavish display when they are in bloom that they are well worth planting as specimens.

And then there are a few roses that are tidy in their growth habits and have good qualities of hardiness and continuous bloom, but that are undistinguished as far as the form of the individual blossoms is concerned: for example, most of the polyanthas and such shrub roses as

Otto Linne and Sea Foam, both of which provide a continuous show but are more attractive in the mass than individually.

Shrub roses can be treated much as one would handle other flowering shrubs, such as cydonias, spireas, forsythias, and deutzias. One must be sure to give them sufficient room in which to develop and (except for one or two that prefer poor soil, such as Father Hugo's Rose), deep, well-prepared soil enriched for long fertility. Shrub roses, like all other roses, want at least half a day of sunshine; avoid planting them on the north side of a building, where they would have too much shade.

There is one other consideration about using shrub roses: for the foliage to stay healthy and the bush attractive all summer, nearly all require spraying or dusting, performed at regular intervals. If shrub roses are used in foundation plantings, one should be careful not to get them so close to the building that it will become impossible to spray them from behind when the bushes attain their full stature. Similarly, a question of convenience arises: it can become quite a chore to spray a number of shrub roses dispersed all over a property. You are much better off—and the shrub roses will get sprayed more regularly—if you plant them in the general vicinity of the rose beds.

The term "hedge" is pretty loosely used: we apply it to tidy, low-sheared rows of box and privet, and to tall, unsheared plantings of such shrubs as forsythia and spirea.

Actually, any rose bush can be used for hedging, provided the plants are set close together in a continuous row so that there are no gaps in the planting. Not all roses, however, will make an *attractive* hedge. Most hybrid teas are unsuited for this use. In the first place, most of them do not make a dense enough bush to look good in a hedge; moreover, they need a better circulation of air than can be provided when they are planted very close together. In the absence of air circulation, they may contract either mildew or black spot or both.

Nearly all floribundas and polyanthas have a very bushy, twiggy habit of growth and a rather high resistance to fungus diseases. Problems of air circulation bother them much less than in the case of hybrid teas. These characteristics permit crowding floribundas and polyanthas, and suit them for use in hedges. However, they must not be trimmed geometrically like privet or box. Instead, they should be given a spring pruning to remove dead and unhealthy wood, and then be permitted to grow as they wish. During the growing season, it will suffice merely to pull off the heads of dead blooms with your fingers. This technique will induce a maximum number of flower buds and a better color display than if cutting is undertaken.

Neither floribundas nor polyanthas can be expected to stay healthy in a hedge without regular spraying and watering. The same problem of convenience arises with rose hedges as with shrub roses, but with the added factor of expense involved: to keep a hundred-foot rose hedge sprayed all through the growing season will take an unholy amount of spray, and rose sprays are expensive.

If the foregoing sounds as though I am trying to discourage the establishment of rose hedges, let me correct the misapprehension. Such hedges are lovely and worth having. Nothing, for instance, could be a prettier way to separate a patio from the surrounding lawn than to outline it with a hedge of floribundas. However, one should exercise a little caution and common sense, and not plant such extensive rose hedges that their upkeep would become a burden. Rather than planting a rose hedge all around the yard, you might try something more modest: perhaps a little rose hedge to follow and outline the front walk, or to parallel the driveway turning circle.

Any of the lower-growing floribundas that are suitable for planting in containers are also useful for hedging, but the expense of such a hedge—the roses of which should be planted about eighteen inches apart—will be considerable. Current prices for floribundas vary from about $8.00 to $10.00 for three plants. A hedge about thirty feet long would need twenty-one plants, and would cost somewhere between $56.00 and $70.00. Compare this with privet, which should cost not more than $.25 a running foot!

A less expensive and very effective hedge can be made of the old polyantha, The Fairy, which is astonishingly hardy and literally covers itself with clusters of small pink flowers like those of an old-fashioned rambler. The bushes make such a large spread that they can be set about three feet apart and still produce a continuous hedge. Don't use this one, however, if you can't accommodate the width of the plants: the resulting hedge will be three or four feet wide.

If money is a serious consideration, you can make a hedge of The Fairy at very low cost if you will take the time to raise plants from cuttings, as described in Chapter XI. All you will need is to plant one bush, costing you about three dollars, and take cuttings from it. The Fairy does beautifully on its own roots, and since it is not covered by a plant patent, you are at perfect liberty to try this if you wish. As a matter of fact, you can probably produce a denser hedge from own-root plants of this rose than from budded plants, such as you would obtain from a nursery, as it loves to put up extra stems from the roots.

Nurseries specializing in old roses can supply such musk roses as Robin Hood and Will Scarlett, and such hybrid rugosas as Delicata, F. J. Grootendorst and Pink Grootendorst. Again, all of these roses can easily be rooted from cuttings, and none is patented. If I were using any of these, I would set the plants about three feet apart. All of them will make fine hedges, some taller than others. All will need room to accommodate the spread of the plants, which, as in the case of The Fairy, will be considerable—from three to perhaps five feet. On the other hand, they will call for singularly little attention— a generous, early-spring feeding, regular watering, and very occasional spraying.

Incidentally, if you should plant a hedge of musk roses or hybrid rugosas, you will get an added bonus: gather the hips in late summer and early fall and make jelly of them, treating them as though they were crab apples. Actually, roses and apples belong to the same family. You will find the jelly delicious.

I have avoided mentioning one sort of hedge rose till the last, so that it would be most strongly brought to your attention. *Rosa multiflora*, which has its legitimate rose-garden use as an understock for budded plants, is widely advertised as a hedge rose, usually under the name Living Fence. *Don't* buy it, unless you are a farmer who wants a substitute for barbed-wire fences. Under favorable conditions—and most conditions appear to be favorable to it—this rose will make a bush eight feet tall and ten feet through. In early summer it is covered with tiny, single white blooms, after which it bears quantities of little red hips. These the birds find irresistible, and the undigested seeds are scattered far and wide in the birds' droppings. These seeds, already partly softened by the birds' digestive juices, and handily premanured, usually germinate where they fall. I have observed that pastures surrounded with multiflora hedges are soon full of volunteer plants. A multiflora hedge makes an almost impassable barrier, one of the thorniest, densest growths one could imagine, so prickly and solid that cattle and horses won't try to push through it once it gets established. It makes wonderful cover for all kinds of wild creatures: rabbits, partridges, pheasants, quail, and songbirds of all sorts, supplying them with both shelter and food. On farms and large country estates it has a valuable purpose to fulfill, but it does *not* belong in your front yard.

Using Roses as Ground Cover

Not many home owners will have occasion to use roses as ground cover. The few varieties that have a supine habit of growth take up a great deal of ground space when they get established, as all of them are rampant and make very long canes. However, this very characteristic makes them valuable to people whose properties have banks or other untidy areas where grass won't grow, and which are too steep or inaccessible for easy gardening. Some of these ground-cover roses, moreover, tend to take root at various places along the canes where they come in direct contact with the ground, and from these growth nodes the plants produce additional sets of canes, so that soon a large area will be covered with a solid mat of rose canes.

Most rambler roses can be employed as ground cover; by comparison with other climbers, ramblers have very lax, flexible canes that would just as soon lie on the ground as climb on a support. Ramblers put up a large number of canes from the base of the plant, a useful trait in a ground-cover plant. Few rose nurseries still handle ramblers; they have been largely replaced by everblooming climbers. However, some of the firms that specialize in old roses still offer them. Some of the better varieties are American Pillar (pink and white); Crimson Rambler; Queen of the Prairies (pink); and Etain (apricot-pink). The last mentioned has the happy faculty of repeating bloom.

If I were going to plant a bank or other awkward spot with ramblers, I would space the plants about five or six feet apart each way. They put out such remarkably long canes that they should soon fill in the blank spaces. Their natural tendency to root where the canes touch the ground can be assisted by pegging and layering, techniques that I shall describe presently, after I have mentioned a few other roses that can be used as ground cover.

There are at least two species roses that make fine ground cover, having a habit of growth much like that of ramblers: *Rosa soulieana*, which bears quantities of small, single white blooms; and *Rosa wichuraiana*, sometimes called the Memorial Rose, which also has white, single blooms. I would handle them as though they were ramblers. To find either, you should write to a nursery specializing in old roses.

All of the ground-cover roses that I have mentioned so far are quite hardy and can be grown where the winters are severe. Persons who live in mild-climate areas can grow two rather tender roses that make especially good ground cover: the Cherokee rose, actually a species rose from China, *Rosa laevigata;* and Mermaid, a hybrid of *Rosa bracteata.* The Cherokee rose has large, single pink blooms, borne very profusely in a single annual flowering, and is remarkably vigorous in growth. Mermaid has tremendous single flowers of a bright yellow, which it bears repeatedly; it, too, is noted for its extreme vigor. As both of these roses make strong growth and have very long canes, I would plant them six to eight feet apart. Again, it may be necessary to try several specialists in old roses in order to locate either of these varieties.

The shrub rose Sea Foam, which I mentioned previously, can also be used very successfully as a ground cover. However, since it does not make very long canes, it needs to be planted rather close, which involves the purchase of a lot of bushes. Recommended planting distance is two to three feet each way. Its principal recommendation is that it is seldom out of bloom from early summer to late fall, producing great mounds of small white flowers.

Another excellent ground-cover rose, which you may also find hard to locate, is the hybrid rugosa Max Graf, described previously. It is utterly hardy and dependable, has the typical rugosa foliage, and bears one annual crop of great, single pink blooms, like gigantic peach blossoms. This is another unpatented rose (which you are at liberty to multiply from cuttings) that does wonderfully well on its own roots. To obtain rapid coverage of an unsightly area, they may be crowded as closely as a foot apart. However, I would suggest spacing them about three or four feet apart and pegging down the canes as they develop.

Which brings me to the old and interesting technique for multiplying trailing plants known as "layering."

Take some wire coat hangers and cut them into foot-long pieces with a pair of stout pliers. Bend each piece into a giant hairpin shape. You now have a device that can be stuck into the ground over a trailing rose cane so as to keep it in tight contact with the soil. Besides the hairpin gadgets, you will need a sharp pocketknife, some toothpicks or wooden matches, something to dig with, some bricks or flat stones, and a small package of rooting hormone, either Rootone or Hormodin. (These rooting hormones, which stimulate root growth, can be found at garden centers. You can do without them, but you'll do much better with them.)

Select a cane and, at a point two or three feet from its point of origin, where it can be *easily* pressed down to make contact with the ground, slit the underside on a slant, halfway through with the knife. Gently spread the cut open and sprinkle a little rooting hormone powder into the cut. Wedge the cut open with a piece of tooth-pick or matchstick, so it can't heal back together. Dig up a little patch of earth where the cut part of the cane will contact the ground, then peg the cane down by means of the big hairpin things. Mound a little dirt over the part of the cane that has been slit and water it. Finally, lay a flat stone or brick over the buried part of the cane; the purpose of this operation is to keep the ground moist at that point.

About a month after the operation has been performed, remove the stone or brick; it will have served its purpose. If you have been lucky, the cane will already have started to put out roots at the place where the slit was made, and before long the new roots will cause the plant to put up a new top above the roots. Obviously, if you have a trailing rose that started out with eight canes, you can make eight more plants in a ring around the original plant. If you wish, you can sever the new plant from the parent plant and move it to another location, though there would be little point in doing this if your aim is to achieve a solid ground cover.

This is one of several means of asexual reproduction; and while it is contrary to the plant patent law to perform this operation on any plant protected by a still-valid patent, of the roses suitable for use as ground cover, only Sea Foam is patented. With any of the others, you can layer to your heart's content.

Your chances of success with layering are quite high with all of the roses suitable for ground cover; many of them will take root spontaneously where they touch ground. However, I think your chances will be improved if you perform the operation late in the spring or early in the fall, and will be further enhanced if you work some peat moss into the soil where you propose to layer the cane.

Planting a steep bank with roses is not particularly easy. In the first place, the soil is usually thin and poor on banks. I would dig a large hole for each rose bush and replace poor, rocky soil with good topsoil, liberally mixed with peat moss and enriched with bone meal. Then, to discourage erosion, I would make a little retaining wall just below each rose bush. The easiest way to accomplish this is get some stout stakes and some boards about a foot wide; cut the boards into three-foot lengths and put one on edge below each bush, securing it with a couple of stakes. Extra earth can then be piled in behind each board, creating a sort of miniature terrace for each bush. By the time the boards and stakes rot away—which should be in two or three years—the bushes should be well established.

V I I I

Making Rose Beds

THE first problem in preparing a suitable rose bed lies in deciding where to put it. As was discussed in the previous chapter, the location of a rose bed should have some logical and reasonable relationship to existing features of the property, such as the line of a drive or walk, a boundary line, or the orientation of the walls of the house. Most properties have several possible sites for planting, all of them aesthetically pleasing. How, then, should one decide on a particular site in preference to the others?

Here are some questions, the answers to which will dictate your decision.

1. WILL THE ROSES BE FREE OF HARMFUL COMPETITION? Trees or fast-growing shrubs too near to the rose bed will soon invade it to get their roots into the rich, lavishly watered soil. Among the worst offenders are elm, poplar, willow, and privet. Imagine the shadow that each tree would cast if the sun were directly overhead

and try to keep the rose bed twenty feet or more outside of the shaded area.

2. WILL THE ROSES GET ENOUGH SUN? In most places roses need about five or six hours of sun daily if they are to flower well; if they are grown in all-day shade, they will either die or limit themselves to making leaves. About a half-day of direct sunshine is all that roses need if they are grown in temperate or very warm areas with a long growing season. In fact, full sunshine all day in such areas can be as hard on roses as it is on people; both will do better with a little shade, particularly during the long, hot afternoons. In far northern areas, however, where the growing season is comparatively short, it would be better to locate rose beds where they will get full sunshine from dawn to sunset.

3. WILL THE ROSES BE SHELTERED FROM DAMAGING WINDS? During the summer months, when rose bushes are heavy with flowers and foliage and most susceptible to breakage, thunderstorms accompanied by violent winds are most common. Since these summer storms usually appear from the same quarter, a little fore-thought should enable you to locate rose beds where the force of the wind will be broken by some feature of the site, such as a hedge or fence, trees, or a building.

4. WILL THE ROSES BE SHELTERED FROM DRYING WINDS? In some areas, particularly where the land is very flat and far from any large body of water, the wind blows steadily, day after day, from morning to night. Such winds tend to dry out people, animals, and plants alike, and roses suffer particularly. A rose bush in bloom and in good condition is rather succulent, the leaves and stems being full of moisture. Alter this condition and the blooms will be poor and the plant unthrifty. Heavy

watering and deep mulching will help greatly to combat the drying effects of winds, but a still more effective method of protection is to plant the roses where some feature of the site, such as a building, a wall, or a hedge, will deflect the wind from the rose beds.

5. WILL THE ROSES BE PROTECTED FROM HARMFUL WINTER WINDS? One should be aware of two potential sorts of damage from winter winds: possible loosening of plants in the ground and possible freezing of the canes. Because the soil gets soft with winter rains in areas where hard freezes are rare, winter winds can cause excessive shaking and buffeting of the rose bushes, resulting in the roots being loosened. This condition is very bad for the plants, and may cause them to die.

In areas of severe winter cold, winds can augment the effect of low temperatures. As anyone knows, it is easier to endure a cold day when the air is still than when a brisk wind is blowing. And even though you may protect your rose bushes with straw and special wrappings, they will have a better chance of coming through a severe winter if they do not also have to endure freezing winds.

6. IS THE PROPOSED SITE REASONABLY LEVEL? A rose bed can be established as a sort of level step or terrace running parallel with a slope, but it should not be made to run up and down the slope. It is a question of irrigation. If all the water runs to one end, the lower end will be too wet, the upper end too dry, and none of the bushes will do well. However, minor irregularities in the level of a site can be corrected with the use of permanent bed edging. In fact, the improved watering that results from installing permanent bed edges is one of the best arguments for their use.

7. WHAT KIND OF SOIL IS AT THE PROPOSED SITE? Poor soil can be removed bodily from the area of a rose bed and good soil put in to replace it. But this is a last-resort sort of measure, to be avoided whenever possible, if only for reasons of expense.

Take a shovel and do a little digging where you propose to establish your rose bed. Can you dig down eighteen inches before you start to encounter many rocks? Do you have several inches of topsoil? What kind of subsoil do you find? If it turns out to be a mixture of heavy clay and rocks, you may have trouble with drainage; water will lie on top of such soil and soak into it with agonizing slowness. On the other hand, if the soil seems to be largely sand, loose and crumbly, you may have drainage problems of a reverse nature: water will run through it as fast as it is applied, leaving the soil around the roots of your roses continually dry.

Either a very heavy or a very light subsoil may be subject to some degree of correction; this problem is not crucial, but should be given some consideration in selecting a site for a rose bed.

Preparing the Bed

Having selected a site, you should proceed to lay out the bed. What dimensions to use will be decided on the basis of several factors, the most important of which will be how many rose bushes you want the bed to accommodate, as previously discussed in Chapter VII.

For the sake of illustration, let us assume that you live in a temperate part of the country and that you want to make a bed that will accommodate a dozen rose bushes selected from the better hybrid teas and floribundas. (Incidentally, if you are new to rose growing, a dozen bushes is a good starting number—enough to make a charming display, but not so many that maintenance of the bed will become a serious chore.)

You could, if you wanted, plant your roses in single file, spacing them two feet apart; in which case you would have to make a bed about twenty-six feet long and about two feet wide. The resulting bed would be inartistic, but would serve the needs of the bushes in terms of growing room.

A better effect would be secured if you made the bed only half as long and twice as wide, so as to accommodate a double row of bushes. If the roses are properly spaced in the bed, the double rows will be as easy to tend as bushes would be in single file. However, you should not be tempted to do a three-row planting; my experience is that the roses in the middle row will be very hard to tend and will, consequently, be neglected.

From the foregoing, it would appear that our dozen roses will need a bed about thirteen feet long by four feet wide. And indeed, such a bed will accommodate the bushes nicely. For convenience, I suggest that it be made rectangular.

Provide yourself with half a dozen short stakes, a ball of mason's twine, a hammer, a yardstick, and a large grocery carton.

Let us suppose that the new bed is to parallel a walk, and is to be separated from it by a two-foot-wide strip of lawn.

The first step will be to lay out the edge of the bed nearest the walk. Decide on the location of one corner two feet in from the edge of the walk and drive a stake at that point. Tie a loop of twine around the stake at ground level and unreel about fifteen or twenty feet of string. Pull the twine taut and temporarily drive a second stake two feet from the edge of the walk. Wind several turns of string around the stake so that it will stay stretched for the time being. Now measure off thirteen feet accurately from the first stake and drive your second corner stake at the thirteen-foot mark, touching the twine; remove the temporary stake and wind the twine around the new corner stake, pulling the twine taut.

You now have established one side of the bed by means of a taut string fastened to two stakes thirteen feet apart and uniformly two feet distant from the edge of the walk. Now you must make a right angle and establish one of the ends of the bed.

Do not cut the twine where it is attached to the second corner stake. Instead, unwind about six or seven feet from the ball of twine and extend it approximately at a right angle. After wrapping a few turns of twine around a spare stake, check the angle by making use of the grocery carton, which is accurately rectangular. Drive the stake when you have the angle precisely established, then measure off the four-foot distance accurately along the twine and drive the third corner stake. Proceed by this method to lay out the thirteen-foot back line of the bed and the other four-foot end. You will end up with four corner stakes joined with a continuous taut string.

I assume that the area where you have staked out your proposed rose bed will be in turf, for the very good reason that most people establish lawns before they plant flowers. You will have to dig up the grass and its roots and get rid of it before you start turning up the soil to make the rose bed. Otherwise, you will be plagued for years with grass coming up in the rose bed.

Using the taut twine as a guide, thrust a square-ended spade into the ground to a depth of about four inches all around the bed, then make additional cuts to divide the turf into manageable squares. (If you have an edger, it is a little easier to use in turf cutting than a spade.) Then, using a spading fork, work horizontally under the turf at a depth of about two inches to lift off the square of turf. Pile the turf away from the bed as you remove it. The more cleanly you take up the grass at this time, the less weeding you will have to do later.

Assuming that you have a depth of several inches of topsoil, and subsoil that is not too rocky or obdurate in consistency, your next job is to break up the ground to a depth of a foot or more, remove any large rocks, roots, or other unwelcome objects encountered in the digging, and work a lot of peat moss and bone meal into the soil. Some dried cow or sheep manure would be a good idea, too.

If you are feeling energetic, you can do the digging with a spade or a spading fork, driving the implement vertically into the ground as deeply as it will go and upending each spadeful so as to turn the soil over and break up all the lumps. Personally, I had my fill of this sort of activity while serving in the army. A more modern method is to use a rotary cultivator. If you are going to do a lot of gardening, you should own one, but I won't try to convince you of this fact. Rent one for this job and let *it* do the convincing. You should be able to locate a machine fairly easily: hardware stores often have them to rent; tool rental stores have them regularly, and garden centers occasionally. To work up a bed of the size we have decided on, thirteen feet by four feet, you will need the tiller for less than an hour.

When all the turf has been removed, go over the entire bed area once with the tiller, letting it dig as deeply as the machine will work. Then use a rake to get the bed reasonably level. Now spread a layer of peat moss on top of the broken soil, along with some bone meal, and if possible, some dried manure.

For the peat moss I would recommend Canadian sphagnum peat, one full bale (six cubic feet) for a bed of the size contemplated.

If you can't get the Canadian moss, either German or Danish sphagnum moss will work equally well. My only objection to these is that to save on the long overseas shipment, the moss is dried severely and baled very tightly, making it a little difficult to spread. In the absence of sphagnum moss, you may be able to get Michigan peat, an excellent sort. Buy about a hundred pounds of it, and plan to use it all.

In the matter of bone meal, you should have ten pounds for a bed of this size. Bone meal is an almost perfect fertilizer for roses, never burning or otherwise damaging the roots of the bushes. I think it also does things for the flower colors, though I can't prove this. In any case, roses like bone meal, thrive on it, and never seem the worse for it. It is one of the longest lasting of all fertilizers, improving the fertility of a bed for many years.

I mentioned that it would be a good idea to add some dried cow or sheep manure. My reason for suggesting this is primarily because the presence of some manure in the rose bed will do two things for you: encourage the growth of soil bacteria and promote the development of earthworms. Both are necessary for good plant growth: the bacteria to help break fertilizer down into forms that the roses can utilize; the worms to burrow in the soil and let air and water into the bed. I'd provide about twenty-five pounds of dried manure to add to the soil in the bed. This should be enough to be effective, but too little to do any harm.

Supposing now that you have gone over the bed once with the rotary cultivator, turned it deeply, and then leveled it with a rake, your next step is to start spreading the soil additives on top of the bed. Strew the peat moss on the soil as evenly as you can till the whole bale is used up. Then sprinkle the bone meal over the peat moss, and finally spread the dried manure on top of everything else.

Then take the rotary cultivator and go over the whole thing. The rotating tines of the machine will work all of these ingredients deep into the soil, and by the time you have gone over the bed two or three times they will have become so intimately mixed with the soil that you will no longer be able to detect them.

Once you have got the bed to this condition and have raked the soil level (incidentally, final leveling is best accomplished with the edge of a board about four feet long), the best thing you can do is to let the bed sit for a few weeks or months. (This is one very valid argument for making rose beds in the fall and planting them in the spring.) Let the rain pelt on it, let the snow fall on it, let the soil settle. Freshly cultivated soil gets fluffed up like sifted flour. Give it time to settle down and find its proper level before you start planting. The first heavy rain may lower the depth of soil in the bed as much as two inches.

At this point, while the bed is still unplanted, is the most opportune time to install edging, which serves many purposes. It helps to keep grass and other vegetation from growing into the rose bed and stealing food and water from the roses. It provides an aesthetically pleasing transition from the lawn to the bed, a guide for the eye. Most importantly, however, it establishes the boundaries of the bed and provides a visual reference against which to judge the level of the soil. If the soil in the bed is kept reasonably level, watering will also be reasonably uniform, and the rose bushes will prosper.

What to use for edging? This question is more easily answered negatively than positively. Don't use roll metallic edging, whether aluminum or steel. It is a nuisance. When you are cultivating the rose bed, your cultivator or rake will catch on the edging and uproot it. This causes much bad language. When mowing next to the rose bed, the rotary mower blade may catch the metal edging imbedded in the ground and yank it out. It may then, if this is your unlucky day, proceed to whirl the length of strip metal around like a horrid flail—with what damage I leave you to imagine. Even if these things don't happen, one day you are going to kneel prayerfully to tend your roses, plant your knee on the sharp edge of the metal, and cut the devil out of yourself, a contingency too horrid to contemplate. Use something else.

Redwood or chemically pressure-impregnated rot-resistant lumber make a good edging. You will need two-by-six planks and two-by-two stakes of the same wood. Use a trowel or shovel to dig a shallow trench all around the perimeter of the bed. Then set the planks on edge in the trench, nailing them to the stakes with coated nails. The stakes should be inside rather than outside the bed for best appearance and easiest mowing around the bed. In the corners, it may be advisable to use paired stakes, or two-by-four stakes. A carpenter's level should be used to make sure that the edging is set as near level as possible, so as to facilitate earth leveling and watering.

Many rose growers, having determined the final and permanent position of a rose bed, choose to surround it with a low cement curb to serve as an edging. This becomes merely a matter of constructing a simple form and pouring cement, which you can do yourself or hire done. In cold climates it may be necessary to first lay down a six-inch-deep layer of gravel as a foundation and to cast the curbing in two-foot lengths to protect it from cracking, always a possibility where heavy winter frosts prevail. In milder climates, however, this may be wholly unnecessary. Personally, I would suggest getting the advice of a competent building contractor.

As an alternative to poured cement, use an edging constructed of cement blocks, either laid free or mortared together. I think the solid two- or four-inch-thick blocks look better than the ones that have holes in them, and tinted blocks are better than cement-colored ones. However, you can always paint them with cement paint.

Many people find ordinary bricks the handiest and most pleasing material for bed edging. My experience is that a good semipermanent edging can be made by setting bricks on end in a shallow trench dug all around the bed. The bricks should touch one another and protrude about half of their length from the ground. After the bricks are in place, tamp the earth against them with the end of a piece of two-by-four.

I have yet to see the rose bed that didn't do better after it was edged than it had before. Even so, it would be worth doing it only for the sake of appearance.

If you intend to plant any climbing roses, you will almost surely wish to make individual planting sites for each rose, the reason being that climbers should be spaced six to eight feet apart. Instead of making a continuous bed to contain the climbers, it is common practice to make a series of small beds, each large enough to accommodate just one rose bush. For this, I suggest making each planting site two feet by three feet. In each site I would use about two bucketfuls of peat moss, a pound of bone meal, and about half a bucket of dried manure. You can use an ordinary two-gallon water bucket to measure the manure and moss.

I X

Planting Roses

FALL planting—particularly of bare-root bushes—is very popular in some northern areas. The bushes are set out just before the onset of winter. Since the nurseries do not dig and store their bushes until well into the autumn, these fall-planted bushes are of the current crop and are about as fresh as possible.

Fall planting works well in areas where the climate will cooperate. Since the bushes must not break dormancy until the first warm days of spring, there must be no midwinter thaws to start growth, which would promptly be killed as soon as cold weather recurred. There should be ample rain late in autumn after the roses have been planted or water must be supplied, so that the ground will be damp enough to promote root growth during the winter: the root system will often go right on growing long after the tops have gone dormant. Soil should be hilled up over the canes of the new bushes and not removed till spring. Finally, there should be a good covering of snow to further insulate and protect the plants. In places like Michigan or southern Ontario, where winter starts early and usually stays in business till April, fall planting will work very well. Come spring, the fall-planted bushes are well established and have put out an impressive root system. But in an erratic climate like that of Tennessee—I've known the temperature to be in the seventies on New Year's Day and hit ten degrees the day following—fall planting can be a chancy business.

Winter planting of container-grown roses is common in subtropical areas such as central Florida, where the winters are so mild that few plants really go into dormancy. Some bare-root roses are planted there, particularly in the late fall—the stores carry a few—but the preponderance of roses planted in central Florida come in gallon cans, with roots in soil and a full set of leaves.

In most of the rest of the United States, mid-spring is the favored rose-planting time, usually coinciding cheerily with the blooming of forsythia bushes and Darwin tulips. And the roses that are planted are either bare-root bushes shipped from the nursery where they were grown, or stored, packaged bushes.

There is really no trick to planting a container-grown rose bush, once the soil in the bed has been made ready. Slit the tin or other container in which the bush is planted to facilitate removing the bush without breaking the ball of earth on the roots. Dig a hole in the bed at least the size and depth of the container, lift out the bush, and put it in the hole at the same depth as it was growing in the container. Pull earth in around the root-ball and flood the site with water.

If you have bare-root bushes, the planting procedure is a bit more complex, but not greatly so.

Let us suppose that you have to plant a dozen bare-root roses just received by parcel post from a nursery. Let us further assume that the rose bed is already prepared, and that the weather is suitable for planting.

The roses have been shipped in a large cardboard container. You open it and find an inner container consisting either of a clear plastic bag or of a wrapping of a special kraft paper that is coated on one side with a black plastic film. Inside are the rose bushes. Their roots are bare, their tops are tied together with string, and each bush carries a name tag. The inside surface of the inner container is dotted with drops of water, and the rose bushes look moist and rather succulent. If the weather has been notably warm while the roses were in transit, the probability is that some or all of them will be showing a few new shoots on the canes, perhaps half an inch long.

While the bushes can be planted immediately, they will do better if they are given a preliminary soaking. Fill a tub or some buckets with water; for each gallon of water, dissolve one tablespoon of any of the following plant foods: Ortho Liquid Plant Food, Ra-Pid-Gro, or Hyponex. Place the rose bushes in the water, spreading out the roots. Make sure the whole root system is immersed. Leave them in a cool place, out of direct sunshine, and let them soak for twenty-four hours, more or less. Should rain or some other emergency delay planting, the bushes could soak for an extra day or even two without damage.

Sometimes everything seems to conspire to keep you from planting some newly bought rose bushes. I've known a sudden freeze, late in the spring, to interrupt planting; or there may be torrential rains. Should this happen, take the box of roses, packed the way it was when it left the nursery, and talk your local grocery manager into letting you store the box in his produce room. This is a refrigerated room where things like lettuce and apples are kept at a temperature just a few degrees above freezing. I've stored roses this way for as long as two weeks without hurting them. Lacking a friendly grocer, if you must hold roses for planting, your best bet is to bury them. Remove all wrappings from the plants, dig a hole big enough to accommodate the bushes, and bury them completely, tops and all. You can keep them this way for two weeks or so.

But let us suppose you are lucky; the weather is warm and dry, and your roses have finished soaking. If you had only one rose bush to plant, I would tell you to dig a hole about two feet in diameter, wide enough to spread out the roots, and deep enough to plant the bush. But you have a dozen bushes to set out in the same bed in two rows of six plants, accurately spaced. I have found the individual-hole method singularly awkward for planting a number of bushes in a symmetrical arrangement, and prefer planting them in trenches.

Start at the back of the bed and dig a continuous trench about a foot in from the back edge of the bed. Make it as wide as the shovel blade and about six inches deep. Pile the soil down the middle of the bed.

Before you plant, take time to examine one of your rose bushes. You will note that it has a rather short, stocky trunk, terminating at the lower end in a pronounced crotch and a number of roots, some of which may be two feet or more long. At the upper end of the trunk there are three or four stout canes tied together at their tops. All of these canes grow from a knobby bulge on the side of the trunk, almost at the top. This bulge is known as the "bud union"; it is the most important part of your rose bush. It is the place where, in the course of raising the bush for the market, the nursery took a little piece of wood and bark containing a live eye or bud from the fancy variety—Mister Lincoln or Peace or whatnot—and grafted it to the trunk of a rose bush of another variety, probably multiflora or Dr. Huey. This eye, once established on the understock, proceeded to grow mightily, nourished by the alien roots of its foster parent, whose original top was cut off to force growth and vigor into the eye. You can see the stub where the original top was removed; it will be on the opposite side of the trunk from the bud union.

So long as the eye is not frozen or damaged, it will continue to grow vigorously and will put out a whole new bush top, which will bear flowers like those of the plant from which the eye was taken.

Now that we know something about the anatomy of rose bushes, let's get back to planting. Prune off any broken or damaged parts of the roots on all of the bushes.

Take one of the bushes and set it in the trench, about a foot from the end of the bed. Estimate the planting depth; when the soil is replaced, the bud-union knob should generally be covered about an inch deep (see page 157 for exceptions). If the knob is too low, pull a little loose soil into the trench and sit the bush on top of it; if it is too high, dig out some more. After you have planted a few roses, this operation will become almost automatic. Make sure that the roots are spread up and down the length of the trench. When the depth appears right, pull some soil in to cover the roots and pack it down till the bush will stand. Now set a second bush in line with the first, following the same procedure, and continue till six bushes have been set in place.

To assure even spacing of your bushes, cut a stick as long as the distance you wish to have your bushes separated and use it to check the placement of each bush. It is much faster than using a yardstick.

You should encounter little difficulty in setting six bushes in the trench dug in the back of the bed. Some of the bushes may have had very long roots: these you will have spread out longitudinally in the trench. If they happened to overlap the site of the next bush, no matter. Bushes so planted will do much better than bushes whose roots have been severely pruned or bent to conform to the sides of a planting hole. Herein lies the principal advantage of trench planting: you always have room for the roots.

When all six roses have been set in the trench, fill it half full of soil and tramp the soil down hard with your feet. Then turn a slow stream of water from the hose into the trench and fill it with water. Let the water drain away and then fill in the rest of the soil, but don't tramp it down.

A second trench should be dug in front of the bed and the same planting procedure followed. In setting this row of bushes, you will gain a little extra room if you stagger the plants in relation to those in the back row (see Figures 1, 2, and 3).

When the whole bed has been planted, snip the strings holding the tops together and scrape up loose earth from the center and edges of the beds, mounding it up over the tops of the bushes. If necessary, bring some extra soil and pile it around the bushes until only three or four inches of the canes are showing. If a few long canes stick out farther, don't worry about it.

When the bushes have been planted, check on them daily. If it hasn't rained, water them, letting the hose flow slowly on the ground between the plants. In spring planting, watch the tips of the canes protruding from the mounds of earth. In a couple of weeks, they will begin to sprout. That is the time to start removing the soil mounds, a little at a time, till the bushes are uncovered to the original level of the bed.

As you remove the soil of the mounds, you will find under the sheltering earth tender new growth, easily broken. I find that the safest way to take down the mounds is with a gentle stream of water, and I like to spread out the process of uncovering over a week or more.

If you are of an inquisitive turn of mind, you probably want to know the reason for mounding the new plants. The principal reason is to keep the tops from becoming desiccated by sun and wind before the roots can become established. Buried in moist soil, the canes remain soft and succulent, and the new growth of buds and shoots is protected from too sudden exposure to the elements.

How deeply rose bushes should be set in the ground depends largely on the climate where they are to grow. In very mild areas, where winter freezes are rare and light, roses are usually planted shallowly, with the bud union an inch or more *above* the surface. In areas of severe winter weather, however, the bud union is best buried an inch or so deep, so that it will have added protection against freezing.

Occasionally you may have own-root bushes to plant,

that is, bushes that are not grafted to an understock. This is how some shrub roses and almost all miniatures are produced for the market. Such plants should be set in the ground to the depth at which they were grown in the nursery. The appearance of the bark of the trunk will serve to indicate the original planting depth.

Most of this process of planting is fairly obvious, and you will acquire proficiency through practice. However, after having planted roses by the hundreds, I have picked up a few tricks that may be worth passing along.

Use your measuring stick to help you judge how deeply you are setting each bush. Merely lay the stick across the soil of the hole or trench to check the level of the bud union in relation to the stick.

As you fill in soil around the roots, make sure that the dirt gets into all of the space around and between the roots and under the root-crotch. Otherwise, damaging air spaces may be left, which may kill the roots. If a bush has a pronouncedly sharp root-crotch, it will be helpful to upend the bush just before setting it and stick a wad of dirt into the crotch, the most likely place for an air space to develop. Your fingers are the best possible tools for tamping the loose dirt around and between the roots as the trench is filled in. The final flooding of the trench with water should get rid of any small air pockets still remaining.

Nearly everywhere in the United States roses will do better if they are deeply mulched after they begin to leaf out. One exception is in a particularly humid, hot climate such as prevails in central Florida. Rose growers there tell me that a mulch may serve as a breeding ground for such damaging fungi as mildew and black spot. However, this is the exception that serves to reinforce the rule.

What to use as a mulch will depend on what is cheap and available locally. Some very popular mulches are pine needles, shredded bark, buckwheat hulls, cocoabean hulls, cottonseed hulls, ground corncobs, salt hay, straw, shavings, and decomposed sawdust. Many people use peat moss for mulching, but I find it generally unsatisfactory; it belongs *in* not *on* the ground. A good mulch won't pack down from its own weight; will allow rain to penetrate to the beds, but will not wash away in a heavy rain (peat moss will float off); will not overheat from decomposition (the main trouble with fresh grass clippings as a mulch); and is cheap enough to use lavishly.

An excellent mulch can be made of dead tree leaves, grass clippings, weed tops, and similar vegetable debris by starting a humus pile. To do this, enclose a circular space, perhaps six feet in diameter, with stakes and chicken wire to a height of about two feet. Inside the enclosed area pile vegetable material, such as dead leaves, in layers about six inches deep, alternating with layers of soil, perhaps two inches thick. Over each layer strew a thin layer of lawn fertilizer. If you can get some stable or chicken manure, add layers of it about two inches deep. Pile until these materials are fairly deep—two feet or more—and make a hollow in the top to hold water. Flood it with the hose. Let this material stand and decompose for several months, till it turns into soft, loamy material. It will attain this state somewhat faster if, after the pile has stood for a couple of months, it is turned over with a fork. The humus that will finally result from this operation is one of the finest materials you can use in gardening: good for potting plants, for turning into the flower beds, or for use as a mulch.

Whichever mulch you use, it should be applied to the rose bed late in the spring so as to cover every bit of the bed to a depth of two inches or more. (The bed should first be deeply cultivated, fully weeded, and heavily watered.) A deep mulch will keep the roots of the roses cool and moist, while the tops are stimulated by the sun. Under these circumstances—cool feet, warm head— a rose bush will grow like mad and bloom astonishingly. The weeds that usually infest the enriched soil of rose beds will be discouraged by the mulch, while the few that make an appearance can be easily pulled up from the moist soil of the bed without breaking their roots. Watering will seldom be needed in areas of reasonable rainfall, as the mulch will retard the evaporation of water from the bed. Next to regular spraying and proper cutting of the blooms, I consider mulching the most important task in caring for roses.

In recent years there have been radical developments in weed and insect control through the application of chemicals to the soil in the beds. A number of selective weed killers have been perfected that, when applied to the soil of a freshly weeded bed, will prevent the germination of any weed seeds that happen to be in the soil. The use of such "preemergent" weed killers, as they are called, is of help in controlling weeds in all sorts of flower and vegetable beds. "Systemic" insecticides have also been developed that, when applied to the soil in a bed, let the plant take them in through the roots to spread through the tops of the plants, where the insecticide will kill chewing and sucking insects. Some are quite effective in the care of roses when package directions are meticulously followed.

If either weed killers or systemic insecticides are to be used, the first application should be made immediately before mulching. Subsequent applications as required, usually once a month, will necessitate removing the mulch or pulling it to one side. A bit of a nuisance, but not too much trouble in view of all the benefits obtained from mulching.

Some mulches, as they decompose on top of the beds, have a bad habit of removing nitrogen from the soil to help in the process of decomposition. Personally, I think that the amount of nitrogen so lost is slight and will seldom cause trouble, but if you want to be doubly sure, you can strew a little lawn fertilizer on top of the mulch.

Everything that I have had to say about planting roses in beds applies equally well to planting them in tubs or other containers. A similar soil mixture containing a generous proportion of peat moss and some bone meal should be used. If the basic soil is a hard clay, it will also be useful to mix in a fair proportion—as much as a quarter of the total bulk—of coarse builder's sand, which will help to keep the soil from packing. To assure good drainage, it is essential to use containers with drainage holes in the bottom, and desirable to use about two inches of gravel in the bottom of the planter. A few handfuls of wood charcoal should be scattered over the gravel to absorb impurities and keep the soil sweet. (Don't use charcoal briquets for this purpose.)

One precaution should be taken. Plants in containers will suffer from drought more readily than those set out in the open ground. Such roses must be carefully watched against drying out and kept thoroughly watered.

X

Caring for Roses

TAKING proper care of roses is about a nine-month job in most parts of the country, and a year-round one in really mild-climate areas.

Wherever you live, rose care starts with the beginning of spring, which may be the first of May in the north or the first of February in subtropical areas.

Cleaning Up

If the rose bushes have been mulched all winter as they should be, the first task is to rake out all of the old mulch and get rid of it; it is best to burn it, in case it harbors fungus spores and insect eggs.

Break up the soil around the plants carefully, so as not to injure the roots, but sufficiently to let air and water penetrate the bed. Pull up any weeds you encounter. If the bushes have been wrapped or winter-protected in any way, remove the coverings and let the sun and air get to them.

Fertilizing

I have found much disagreement among rose enthusiasts in the matter of fertilizing the bushes. If you wish, you may buy a special rose fertilizer and apply it according to directions. I have had excellent results, however, from feeding roses with ordinary farm fertilizers, as follows:

Give each bush a feeding of a fertilizer relatively high in nitrogen. I would suggest using a 15-15-15 or 10-10-10 formula. Strew from one-half to three-fourths of a cup of this fertilizer in a ring around each bush, on top of the soil, keeping it about a foot out from the trunk of the bush. Scratch it lightly into the soil. For a big, well-established climber, I'd use twice as much fertilizer.

After the early spring fertilizing, wait until the roses have made their first burst of bloom and then repeat the feeding with a 6-12-12 formula, applying half a cupful around each bush. Fertilize again late in the summer, as soon as the nights begin to get a little crisp, using half as much of the same fertilizer as on the previous occasion. After the roses have quit blooming and the first early winter frosts have occurred, I think it is helpful to use a final application of a nitrogen-free fertilizer, such as 0-10-10, to promote the continued growth of the root system during the dormant winter period.

Pruning

Spring pruning should next be undertaken, before new growth gets started in earnest.

Use a sharp rose-pruning shears. First cut out all dead canes, starting near the top of the cane and working downward until you reach live, white wood. Make your last cut about half an inch above an eye, cutting on a slant. If it turns out that the whole cane is dead, cut it off flush with the trunk.

Next cut out all diseased wood. Look particularly for canes that show dark brown, purplish, or black blotches on the bark. This is a sign of cane canker. Cut through such canes near the top. If the cane is infected, the wood will be brownish, with tan or yellowish pith. Work down the cane till you get to clean white wood with white pith, as described before. Burn the diseased wood.

Shorten the other canes, even if they are healthy. As a rule of thumb, reduce the bush to about half its former height. Remove any canes that cross others at an angle: they will cause bark damage where the canes rub.

Look for suckers: shoots coming from the understock and always originating *below* the bud union. Trace them to their point of origin and cut them off flush. Otherwise, if they are left to develop, they will starve out and kill the top of the bush. Well-grown bushes from reliable sources, however, seldom develop suckers. When roses are grown on their own roots, of course, this problem does not present itself.

Climbers need special treatment in pruning. Like other roses, they need to have dead and diseased wood removed promptly. How and when the remaining pruning should be done will depend on the sort of climbers to be pruned.

Modern everblooming climbers should be pruned along with the hybrid teas. The main canes and side branches that flowered in the previous year should be pruned: the main canes lightly, so as to shorten them by about one-third, the side branches more severely, so as to leave only three or four eyes on each. Very old canes with hard, tree-like bark should be cut out entirely, so as to allow newer canes to take over. When the bark of a cane becomes very hard, and the wood of the cane keeps on growing, the inner bark layer through which the sap has to flow gets constricted, largely cutting off the circulation of sap in the cane, with a consequent loss of flowering. Such a cane is said to be "bark bound" and is better removed.

As you prune, consider the direction in which the cane will resume its growth: the more nearly horizontally the cane can be encouraged to grow, the better it will flower.

Most of the climbing forms of hybrid teas and floribundas are better not pruned until after they have finished their first big blooming period of the summer. They may then be lightly pruned as just described. The older large-flowered climbers, like Paul's Scarlet, which bloom only once a year, should be treated the same way.

True ramblers, such as Dorothy Perkins and Crimson Rambler, should be pruned drastically immediately after they finish blooming. Canes that have just bloomed should be cut off at the base and newer canes encouraged to take their place.

To prune climbers, you will need a pair of long-handled loppers, as the canes get very large and surprisingly hard. To remove really large, old canes at the base of the bush, a saw will usually be needed.

Painting Cuts

Keep a can of orange shellac or asphalt paint handy, along with a small brush. When you finish pruning a rose bush, dab some shellac or paint on the freshly cut stub to prevent loss of moisture and the possible invasion of the stem by boring insects, which like to burrow in the pith.

Mulching

When you are through pruning, and have the beds cultivated, fed, and thoroughly weeded, put down a deep layer of new mulch. Try to do this before the advent of hot weather.

Regular Preventive Maintenance

Keeping your roses healthy, after the first spring chores have been finished, is largely a matter of the regular, faithful repetition of watering, weeding, fertilizing, clipping, and spraying.

Watering

How often roses will need to be watered will depend on several factors. In damp, rainy areas it may seldom be necessary to irrigate rose beds, but such places are rare. The temperature has a lot to do with it; in hot weather it may be necessary to water twice as often as in cool weather. Sandy soil won't stay wet; rose gardens established in such soil have to be watered almost every day if they are to prosper. Clay soil, on the other hand, is hard to moisten, but once it gets thoroughly wet it will stay wet for days or even weeks.

The way the soil has been prepared for rose planting will have a bearing on how often the bed will need to be watered. If a lot of peat moss, stable manure, humus, or other organic material has been incorporated into the soil of the bed, the need for watering will be reduced, as these materials tend to absorb and hold moisture. In any case, it is always best to be liberal with organic soil additives, regardless of whether your soil is either pronouncedly heavy or light.

Mulching, also, will reduce the need for watering. In areas of reasonable climate where rain is not a rarity, the use of a proper deep mulch may largely obviate the need for frequent irrigating of rose beds.

The test for when a bed needs water is simple: if you can't stick your forefinger its full length into the soil of the bed, it is time to water.

I know two good ways to water roses. One is to remove the nozzle from the hose and let a slow stream run in the bed till the entire bed is soaked, which will require moving the hose frequently. The other way is to use a perforated sprinkler hose or a canvas soaker hose. Run the hose down the center of the bed. In the case of a perforated sprinkler hose, lay it with the holes down. Turn on the water and let it run for an hour or two, till the bed is thoroughly soaked to a depth of about six inches.

A friend of mine, who had several long rose beds, installed a sprinkler hose semipermanently in each bed, holding it in place down the center line of the bed with U-shaped lengths of stiff wire. Then he mulched his beds. He fastened the business end of each sprinkler hose to a stake at the end of the bed, where it could be readily located when he wished to attach a length of garden hose to it. He found the setup very convenient.

However you perform your watering, avoid wetting the canes and leaves of the bushes. Fungus spores are always present on the surface of the soil, and they can easily be transferred to the canes and leaves if the bushes are splashed with a carelessly wielded hose. Failure to observe this precaution is a major cause of black spot infections in rose beds.

Weeding

A properly prepared and deeply mulched bed will require little weeding, as the mulch will tend to inhibit the growth of weeds.

Gardening has a smug, self-satisfied way of teaching its followers object lessons calculated to strengthen and improve their moral fiber. The sin of carelessness in preparing a rose bed will be punished many times over and will be expiated only by constant weeding. Turf turned into the bed, bits of the root system of Bermuda, St. Augustine, and other grasses left in the soil, chunks of dandelion roots—such things will grow with an almost diabolic fervor in your rose beds and keep you weeding all summer.

Failure to install permanent bed edgings will also add to the weeding problem, as the grass from the lawn will promptly invade the rose bed to get to the extra nourishment and moisture.

A related problem may arise from planting roses too close to trees. I remember one of my rose beds that did well for the first year, but was most unsatisfactory in the second year, the roses appearing half stunted. I found that the bed was full of tree roots, and traced them to a winged elm that was more than fifty feet from the bed. I have known a Chinese elm hedge to push roots just under the grass of my lawn and travel more than forty feet to reach flower beds. Poplars are also bad actors in this respect.

Even if you get all of the bits and pieces of grass out of a new rose bed, it is impossible to remove weed seeds that are already in the soil—and turning up the soil to make the bed usually provides just the stimulus that these seeds have been waiting for. Live weed seeds are almost always present in stable manure—though not in dehydrated packaged manure—and will usually germinate after the manure has been added to the soil in the rose bed. I still think, however, that the advantages of using stable manure outweigh the disadvantages, including the extra weeding it may entail.

As I mentioned before, various companies engaged in the production of agricultural chemicals have recently introduced selective weed killers. Some of these have proven themselves to be very useful in reducing the number of weeds in plantings of such vegetables as corn and tomatoes, and a few of them have been used with some success in rose gardens. These latter have been designed to prevent the germination of the seeds of annual weeds.

I have had some limited experience with the chemical

control of weeds in rose gardens, experimenting both in my own plantings and in those of the Municipal Garden. I am still of the opinion that the most generally satisfactory way of combatting weeds is to apply a deep mulch. The weed killers that I tried gave fair protection for a month to six weeks but then had to be reapplied. They were expensive, in comparison with other garden chemicals. And while I cannot prove it, I got the impression that the repeated use of these chemical weed killers had an adverse effect on the rose plants, slowing down their growth and reducing the number of blooms. As I said, I cannot be wholly sure that the weed killers were responsible, but I can't be sure, either, that they weren't. Roses being a rather substantial investment, it might be wise to wait awhile and see what the verdict is about chemical weed killers.

Spraying and Dusting

If I were to attempt to enumerate all of the insects that feed on rose bushes and all of the diseases that plague them, it would require very nearly a whole book. However, they do not *all* come at once or appear in *every* area. There are insects that eat the leaves, others that suck the juices from the young canes and buds, others that bore into the pith of the canes, still others that feed on the petals of the blooms.

One particularly annoying bug, the nearly microscopic rose thrip, squirms between the tiny petals of new, hard flower buds long before they are ready to open and sucks the juices from the base of the petals, with the result that the bud either fails to open at all or produces a rose whose petals are heavily stained with brown.

As for the diseases, most of them are of a fungus nature. There is, for example, black spot, which shows up as black or dark brown circular spots on the leaves, usually starting at the base of the bush. The spots grow larger, and the leaf turns yellow and presently drops. Before you know it the bush is virtually bare of leaves. And there is mildew, a white floury growth that shows up on the leaves, particularly those at the top of the bush, causing them to curl at the edges and roll almost into a tube. Mildew occurs most commonly in cool, damp weather. It is terribly damaging to rose bushes, always weakening them, and may even kill them if it is not checked in time. Not only does it attack the foliage, but it also has a maddening habit of afflicting the stem and base of the just-opening buds, causing the blooms to droop, crook-necked, and the buds to open only half-way. There is also cane canker, which I described earlier, and rust, which looks something like black spot, and a whole host of other diseases.

By now you may be thoroughly discouraged. If you had to treat your rose bushes separately against each of the pests and diseases to which roses are prone, you would have reason to despair, for it would be an endless and hopeless struggle. Luckily, however, it is much simpler than you may think to keep roses healthy. The trick is in the *regular* use of sprays and dusts produced to control insects and fungus disorders.

When I first began growing roses, I had to spray or dust with insecticides and then repeat the process with fungicides. Now, however, there are numerous combination sprays or dusts designed to combat in a single application the insects and fungi that afflict roses. They are all pretty much the same, containing such insecticides as Malathion, Sevin, and lindane, and such fungicides as Captan, Phaltan, and Maneb. Typically, these take the form of a powder to be mixed with water and sprayed on the plants, or a dust to be applied directly with a duster.

I have always found spraying to be more effective than dusting. The wind has to be blowing very strongly to deflect a liquid spray, but the faintest breeze will interfere with dusting. Also, it is hard to avoid inhaling the dust if it is being picked up in the breeze, and since these dusts are designed to kill insects, they are potentially dangerous to humans.

For these several reasons, I rely primarily upon spraying to keep my roses healthy. Spray should be applied at least once a week and not less often than every ten days, if it is to be effective. But even if one is quite regular about spraying, summer rains will wash away the spray residue from the bushes, leaving them open to attack by insects or fungi. Consequently, it is wise to keep on hand some rose dust that can be applied *between* sprayings, when the rain has ceased and the leaves have had time to dry off.

Earlier, I spoke of the use of systemic insecticides. Some of my friends have had very good success with these insecticides, and swear by them. My own reaction to them is mixed. Since you still have to spray for fungus disorders, it is no harder to add some Malathion or Sevin to the spray and get the insects at the same time. Moreover, systemic insecticides are terribly potent chemicals —indeed, some are very toxic—and need to be handled with great care. Personally, I have given up using them.

X I

Asexual Reproduction of Roses

ASEXUAL reproduction is reproduction without sex. Common though it is in the plant world, I find it all but incredible. It seems to me perfectly reasonable that a seed should grow into a radish or an ovum into a senator; but these are familiar and reassuring examples of sexual reproduction, involving the excellent dichotomy of male and female. However, foreign though asexual reproduction is to human experience, it has been known and understood by gardeners in a practical way since primitive times.

There is, for example, an ancient legend concerning Joseph of Arimathea and the Thorn of Glastonbury. Joseph, you will recall, was a wealthy and influential Palestinian Jew who contributed his own tomb for the burial of Jesus after the Crucifixion. According to the legend, he became a disciple and a missionary, found his way into Gaul, and was sent from there to England by the Apostle Philip to found a monastery. Arriving at Glastonbury, near Bath, Joseph decided on a suitable building site and stuck his staff of hawthorn wood in the ground to mark the spot. Amazingly, so the story goes, the staff took root and grew into an immense hawthorn tree, which lived for many centuries and was an object of veneration in the Middle Ages because it bore pink blossoms at Christmas, instead of white ones in May.

It seems probable that there was a venerable hawthorn tree at Glastonbury. It may even have bloomed early and borne pink blossoms—plants have an unexplained way of mutating spontaneously. There is no question that there was a monastery at Glastonbury; it was broken up and the property confiscated by Henry VIII after the separation of the English Church from Rome. All that now remains is a lovely ruin. However, charming as the legend is, there appears to be no truth in it. The monastery was not established until the fifth century, and Joseph of Arimathea had nothing to do with it.

Nevertheless, the fact remains that a freshly cut staff of hawthorn wood might easily take root. The conditions in England—cool weather and plenty of moisture —are ideal for rooting plants. It was probably an accidental discovery at first—the fence post that grew leaves and branches—but it has been common knowledge for centuries that many plants can be reproduced by cutting a short piece of live wood and planting it upright in damp ground. Grapevines have been multiplied this way for thousands of years. When the first European settlers came to this country, they brought not only *seeds* of grain and vegetables and flowers, but also *cut-*

tings of all sorts of trees and vines and bushes, protecting them in layers of damp moss until they could be set out to root in the soil of the New World.

Most of the really remarkable things in this world are commonplaces. Think how astonishing it would be if you could dock a puppy's tail and then grow a second dog from the amputated tip!

Rooting Softwood Cuttings

Asexual reproduction takes many forms, but the use of cuttings is probably the most generally familiar method. You may have seen your grandmother start rose bushes during the winter by rooting cuttings under the protection of a mason jar. The procedure is quite simple, and will work as well today as it did a generation ago.

In the fall, when the nights are beginning to get cool, make cuttings of live branches of roses. The cuttings should be about six to eight inches long, with two or three sets of leaves, and should be taken from the middle part of the branch. (The wood at the tip of the branch is usually too soft to be rooted.) The finished cutting should look something like the sketch in Figure 8 (page 176). About half of the leaves at the upper end should be removed, and the lower end of the cutting should be cut on a long slant with a very sharp knife. All of the leaves should be stripped from the lower half of the cutting. When all of the cuttings have been made, roll them up in a piece of damp newspaper and put them in the bottom of the refrigerator until you are ready to

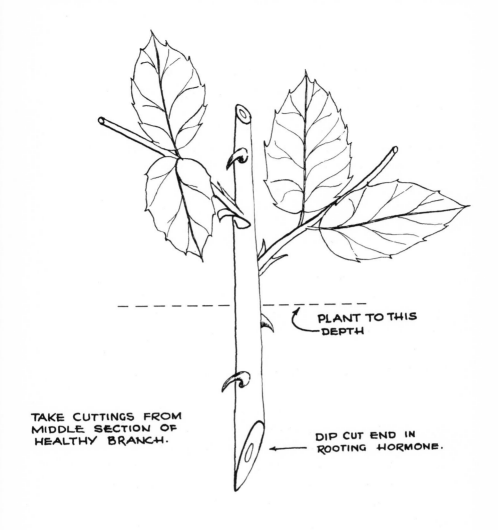

PLANT TO THIS
DEPTH

TAKE CUTTINGS FROM
MIDDLE SECTION OF
HEALTHY BRANCH.

DIP CUT END IN
ROOTING HORMONE.

FIGURE 8.
ROSE CUTTING PREPARED FOR ROOTING

R.A.B.

set them in the ground. They will keep nicely for a week or two if you keep the paper damp.

Now make a nurse bed in which to root your cuttings by digging up a little patch of ground, perhaps two or three feet square, and working sand and peat moss generously into the soil. Be sure to select a site that will have sunshine not more than half the day, and that will be sheltered from prevailing winter winds, if you live in a cold climate.

To root your cuttings, dip the lower end of each in Rootone or Hormodin (powdered rooting hormones that you can buy at any garden store), and then plant the cutting upright, letting about half of its length protrude above the ground. Two or three cuttings can be planted close together. Upend a wide-mouthed, quart-size mason jar over them to serve as a miniature greenhouse, and leave the jar undisturbed until warm weather is established the following spring. By that time, most of the cuttings will have grown roots and started to put out a new top. I find it generally best to make the removal of the jars a gradual operation. They can be taken off during warm spring mornings and replaced later in the day till it seems safe to leave them off entirely. Don't try to transplant the new rose bushes. Let them grow until the following autumn, keeping them well sprayed against disease. It is also best not to let them bloom; remove flower buds as fast as they form. When the autumn nights begin to grow cool, dig up the new bushes, being careful not to break the roots, separate them, and replant them where they are to grow permanently.

Incidentally, while a mason jar will work very well, you will find that a still better miniature greenhouse can be made from a clear-glass gallon jug, the type that Coca-Cola syrup comes in. Any soda fountain will be glad to sell you these jugs.

To make your greenhouse, take a piece of coarse cotton twine, the kind that butchers use to tie up a roast. Dip the twine in kerosene and then tie it around the jug, about an inch from the bottom. Set fire to the twine. When it is about to burn out, dunk the bottom of the jug in a pail of ice water. There will be a snap and the whole bottom of the jug will come off, as neatly as though it had been cut. An alternate method of removing the bottom involves scratching a continuous line around the sides of the jug with a glass cutter, after which you set the jug in the sink, put a funnel in its mouth, and pour in about a quart of boiling water. Wait about thirty seconds, and then turn on the cold water so that it flows around the base of the jug. Off comes the bottom.

Once you have the bottom off, you can set the jug over a group of cuttings the same way as you would a mason jar. The advantages of the jug are twofold. In the first place, it will accommodate several times as many cuttings as a jar. Secondly, if the weather turns suddenly or unseasonably warm, there is no need to remove the jug during the heat of the day; merely unscrew the top to provide ventilation.

You and the Plant Patents Law

Since 1930 it has been possible for the originator of a new variety of a plant to get a patent on it. The patent gives the owner the exclusive rights to the asexual reproduction of the new variety for seventeen years, and the law provides penalties for those who reproduce patented varieties without first getting the permission of the patent holder, even when this is done for personal use. Patented rose bushes are sold bearing a metal tag with the name of the variety and the statement, in fine print, that asexual reproduction of the variety is forbidden. Older varieties are sold without such a tag; instead, the name is usually on an elongated celluloid or cardboard tag fastened around one of the canes.

Actually, if you want to experiment with the asexual reproduction of rose bushes, there are thousands of varieties from which you can choose without breaking the law, and some of them are among the all-time greats—for example, Crimson Glory, Peace, Eclipse, and Charlotte Armstrong, to name just a few.

Own-Root Bushes

Nearly all commercially produced rose bushes are grafted plants, the root system usually being either multiflora or Dr. Huey stock. When you root a cutting of a rose, however, the roots are of the same variety as the top; such a plant is called an "own-root" bush. There was a time, around the turn of the century, when virtually all nursery-grown rose bushes were on their own roots. Now almost no own-root bushes are commercially produced; about the only exceptions are certain hedge roses and miniatures.

Probably the primary reason why almost all rose bushes are grafted is that grafting makes it possible to produce a larger number of bushes from a given supply of budwood. When roses are reproduced by grafting, a single bud or eye is snipped off the parent bush and inserted under the bark of the understock. About the shortest cutting that is practical to use in making an own-root plant will have three or more buds; these same buds would make three or more separate bushes if they were used for grafting.

The secondary reason for the popularity of grafted plants is that some lovely roses do very poorly on their own roots, but thrive when grafted to a suitable rootstock. Why this should be so I don't know, but some varieties just do not produce roots that can do an adequate job of feeding the top. On the other hand, though many nurserymen would disagree with me, it has been my observation that some rose varieties do superlatively well when grown on their own roots: Peace, for example, particularly the climbing form. I have also seen some quite illegally produced plants of Tropicana grown from cuttings, which put to shame grafted plants of this variety.

Own-root plants are particularly desirable, I think, in areas of erratic and severe winters—warm one day, freezing the next. It is sometimes hard to avoid damage to the bud union of grafted plants grown in such a climate. And of course, if the bud union is frozen, you might as well throw away the grafted plant. With an own-root plant, however, even if it freezes to the ground, it will usually make a new top the following spring.

Rooting Hardwood Cuttings

The technique of rooting cuttings under glass requires that relatively new wood be used: neither very soft nor very hard. However, it is also possible to root a section of old cane that is extremely hard, the type of wood that can be found near the base of old climbers.

Remove some canes and branches from the bush early in the fall. Cut them into eight-inch lengths, remove all the leaves, tie them up in bundles of about a dozen, and bury them in a horizontal position at a depth of about a foot in a trench filled with sand. Dig them up in the spring. You will find that most of the cuttings will have developed what is known as a callus on the end that grew lower on the bush: a ring of little white woody knobs or warts. It is from this callus that roots will develop.

Prepare a well-tilled piece of ground in a shady spot, working peat moss and sand generously into the soil so that it becomes loose and crumbly. Plant the callused cuttings about six inches apart, sinking them in the ground to half their length. Water them deeply every day, and in a month or so they will usually take root and develop into strong plants that can be set in their permanent locations in the fall.

The Rubber-Tape Method

If you make inquiries at a hardware store or electrical shop, you can buy a roll of rubber insulating tape known as "splicing compound." This sort of tape is about three-quarters of an inch wide, black or dark gray in color, and is made of very stretchy rubber. One side of the tape is coated with rubber cement, over which there is a glazed cloth backing, which must be peeled off when the tape is used.

Early in the summer, when your rose bushes are in full bloom, select one cane that has two or three strong side branches growing from it. Just below where the side branches come off the cane, perhaps two inches down, make two parallel cuts around the bark of the cane, spacing the cuts a quarter of an inch apart. Try not to cut into the wood, merely through the outer layer of bark. This is delicate work, but you will soon get the hang of it, provided you use a very sharp pocketknife or a razor blade. Remove the outer layer of bark, exposing the white inner layer. Now, take a two-inch piece of the tape, remove the cloth backing, and wrap the tape once around the area where you have girdled the cane, pressing the two ends of the tape together. The tape will stick to itself very nicely.

Forget the cane for a couple of weeks and then observe it daily. Soon you will notice, from the bulging of the tape, that a strong callus is growing at the point where the upper cut was made. Let the callus grow for about three weeks, then strip off the tape, cut off the cane just below the callus (see Figure 9, page 183) and plant the top in a rooting bed as directed for hardwood cuttings.

Properly handled, this method will produce an own-root plant in jig time.

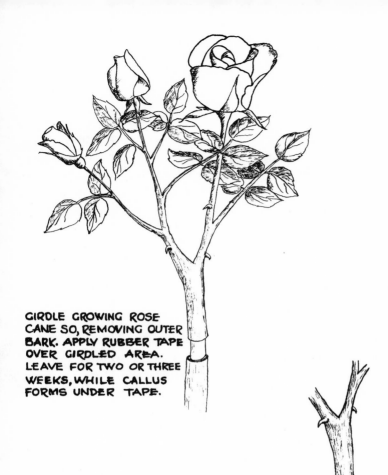

GIRDLE GROWING ROSE
CANE SO, REMOVING OUTER
BARK. APPLY RUBBER TAPE
OVER GIRDLED AREA.
LEAVE FOR TWO OR THREE
WEEKS, WHILE CALLUS
FORMS UNDER TAPE.

APPEARANCE OF GIRDLED
AREA AFTER REMOVAL
OF TAPE. NOTE RING OF
WHITE, KNOBBY CALLUS.
SEPARATE TOP, REDUCE
FOLIAGE 50 PERCENT, &
SET OUT IN ROOTING BED.

CUT HERE

FIGURE 9.

TAPE METHOD OF PREPARING CUTTINGS

R.A.B.

Air Layering

The method known as ground layering, whereby a rose cane is cut partly through and the cut place is buried, has been described in Chapter VII. The method works very well with climbers and ramblers having long, lax canes that can be brought down to the level of the ground. It is almost impossible, however, to use it with roses having an upright growth pattern and stiff canes.

A variation of the technique, known as "air layering," can be used without the branch being bent down to the ground. About midway in the length of a healthy branch or cane, make a long angling cut halfway through the cane, using a sharp knife. Bend the cane slightly so as to open the cut. Sprinkle Rootone or Hormodin into the cut and prop it open with a bit of toothpick or match stick. Now take a handful of wet sphagnum moss, which any florist can sell you, and wad it all around the cut place. Use a piece of clear plastic, such as Saran Wrap, to hold the moss in place, wrapping it around the wad of moss two or more layers deep and tightly fastening both ends around the cane with adhesive tape.

The object of the sphagnum moss is to provide a damp medium in which roots can form. The purpose of the plastic wrap is to keep the moisture from evaporating.

Ultimately, roots should begin to grow in the wad of moss and finally be observable through the transparent plastic. When a good mass of roots has developed, cut off the rooted part of the branch and plant it.

The Constant-Mist Method

Nurseries and greenhouses are increasingly making use of a nozzle designed to produce a spray as fine as fog or mist. These mist nozzles are arranged over greenhouse benches to spray the plants and provide a condition of extreme humidity. Since the spray is so fine, these nozzles use little water: many of them will spray for a whole hour and only use a couple of gallons of water—less than it takes to flush a toilet.

One common cause of failure in attempting to root cuttings is the desiccation of the wood and leaves, a condition that usually results in the death of the cutting. Another common cause of failure is "damping off," a sudden and severe infection of the cuttings with mildew. Strangely, the use of a mist nozzle running almost continuously not only prevents drying out of the leaves and stems of the cutting but tends to prevent fungus infections such as mildew. The latter is thwarted because the mist keeps the plants so constantly wet that mildew spores are washed off as fast as they get on the leaves and stems.

A mist nozzle can be obtained at a cost of about three dollars through greenhouses or plant nurseries, which can order them from dealers in greenhouse supplies. They are equipped with standard threads and will screw onto ordinary pipe fittings.

One way to use a mist nozzle is to arrange a pipe fitted with a nozzle so that it will spray above a rooting bed, prepared in a shady spot as described earlier. It may be helpful to make a screen of clear plastic about two feet tall and arrange it to surround the rooting bed, to keep the wind from blowing the spray away. Keep the nozzle running all day until the cuttings take root.

Another way to use mist nozzles is to select a site that will receive full sun all day, and on it lay out a three-foot square. Enclose the square with boards six inches wide set on edge. Nail the corners together. Now lay bricks inside the enclosure, spacing them about half an inch apart, to form a sort of paving, and spread coarse builder's sand over the bricks to a depth of two or three inches. Attach your mist nozzle to a length of pipe, so contrived with pipe angles that it will overhang the center of the square about two feet above the sand and secure the pipe in place. It is now necessary to construct a vertical frame to enclose the square and the mist nozzle: stakes driven into the ground and joined at the top with a horizontal wire will probably suffice. Finally, drape a large piece of clear plastic over the framework and secure it with string around the wood sides of the square. The kind of plastic sold as a substitute for storm windows will work excellently, and can be obtained at most hardware stores. Attach a garden hose to the pipe with the mist nozzle.

To use the device, make cuttings as shown in Figure 8 (page 176), and stick them in the sand; close the plastic top tightly, and turn on the water. Start the water first thing every morning and let it run till sundown. Cuttings in a rig of this sort will root in astonishingly short order—usually two or three weeks; not only roses, but other things as well, such as lilac, pyrocantha, privet, geranium, magnolia, holly, deutzia, forsythia, and cydonia—just about anything, in fact. Once roots have formed, remove the cuttings to a semishaded location for the balance of the summer.

Bud Grafting

If you want to try bud grafting, you will need to have some suitable rootstock plants already growing. *Rosa multiflora* and Dr. Huey are commonly used for this purpose, although another suitable rose is Ragged Robin, which is used for hedging plants. Any of these will grow readily from cuttings, as previously described. Multiflora can also be grown quite reliably from seeds, taken from well-ripened hips and planted in the open ground. If you live in central or southern Florida, try to obtain some cuttings of the Cherokee rose, and raise it for rootstock. Otherwise, select Dr. Huey.

When you have understock plants growing, cut some branches from a healthy rose bush early in the summer, shortly after the rose has bloomed for the first time in the season. The wood taken, called "budwood," should be of the current season's growth, cut from the middle section of a branch, and reasonably hard.

Examine this wood with care. You will observe that wherever a set of leaves is growing from the branch, at the point where the leaf stem joins the branch there will be a red bud, or eye, hidden in the axilla, or "armpit," of the stem. It is this bud or eye that may be grafted to the understock. If we perform the operation correctly, it will begin growing and will finally develop into a whole new rose bush, nourished by the alien roots of the understock.

With scissors or a sharp knife, cut off the set of leaves,

leaving a half-inch stub of stem. Then take a sharp knife
—a penknife whetted till you can shave the hairs on your
arm—and slice off the bud and leaf stem, removing with
it a thin, shield-shaped layer of bark and wood.

Now take a piece of burlap and wipe clean the bark
of the trunk of the host bush, removing soil, mud, and
some of the smaller thorns from ground level to a height
of three or four inches. Starting about an inch above
ground level, make a vertical slit through the bark about
an inch long. Cross the top of the slit with a second
slit, like the top of a T. Turn back the corners of bark,
using the tip of the knife. You can now slip the shield
of bark down inside the vertical slit; you will find that
the stem stub makes a convenient handle (see Figure 10,
p. 189).

Lap the bark of the host plant over the bud shield and
fasten it firmly in place. Traditionally, this has been accomplished by wrapping the trunk with knitting wool,
strips of raffia, or strips of soft rubber, obtained by cutting apart a soft rubber band. Wool or raffia will have
to be slit in about three or four weeks, so that it will not
strangle the plant; make the cut on the side of the wrapping opposite from the inserted bud. Rubber will rot
off without strangling the trunk.

Some rose nurseries use a special little bandage made
of tape with a hole cut in the center for the bud to stick
through. You can, if you wish, improvise a similar device
from a short piece of splicing compound. I recommend
this method.

About a week or ten days after the bud has been inserted, the stub of stem will wither and fall off. The bud,
or eye, however, should remain a healthy reddish color
and soon should show indications of growing larger. It

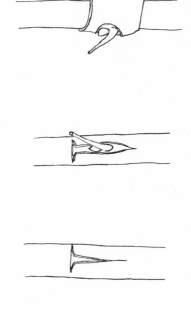

REMOVING BUD SHIELD FROM STICK OF BUDWOOD. RESULTING BUD SHIELD.

TEE-CUT MADE IN TRUNK OF ROOTSTOCK. UPPER CORNERS OF BARK HAVE BEEN PARTLY TURNED BACK. THE BUD SHIELD IS THEN FIRMLY INSERTED INTO THE SLOT, TO BE HELD IN PLACE WITH RUBBER TAPE.

TAPE BEING APPLIED TO HOLD BUD SHIELD. BUD PROTRUDES FROM HOLE IN TAPE. ENDS OF TAPE WILL BE PRESSED TOGETHER. AS BUD GROWS, TAPE WILL STRETCH AND FINALLY ROT OFF.

R.A.B.

FIGURE 10.
STEPS IN BUD GRAFTING

is unlikely that shoots will break from it, however, until the following spring, when the eye should begin to grow into a branch. While waiting for this to happen, keep the grafted plant well cultivated and watered, spray it against insects, and protect it against winter freezes.

When the eye puts forth a stem and leaves, cut off the top of the original host bush about half an inch above the place where the bud eye was grafted. After this season of growing, the grafted plant will be ready to transplant to its permanent location.

There are, of course, refinements to the process. For example, some writers recommend not cutting the top of the host plant off all at once; instead, it is suggested that it be cut half through, and that then the top be bent sharply over toward the growing bud and so left for several months before the amputation of the top is completed. When the eye turns into a growing shoot about two inches long, professional growers often pinch off about half of the shoot so as to force the bud to develop several shoots in place of the original one, thus making a fuller top to the new bush.

Actually, few people will have reason to undertake bud grafting unless they also go into hybridizing, which is discussed in Chapter XII. Once in a while, however, it may happen that you will wish to propagate an old and rare rose variety for your own pleasure; in this case, a knowledge of bud grafting can be extremely useful.

XII

Hybridizing for Fun

I ONCE developed my own rose variety, and for a brief period was its sole proprietor. So satisfying was this experience that ever since I have been promising myself that when I had time, I would pursue rose hybridizing as a hobby. So far, I haven't found the necessary leisure, but I keep hoping.

The rose in question, a deep red hybrid tea, resulted from a chance fertilization of a bloom of Etoile de Hollande. It may have been fertilized through the agency of a questing bee with pollen from another rose, but the chances are fairly high that the rose was fertilized with its own pollen, which happens quite readily.

In any case, one fall day I gathered a ripe rose hip from the bush of Etoile de Hollande, removed the seeds, planted them, and got one seed to germinate. I nursed the little plant in a succession of clay pots and finally planted it in an open rose bed, where it bore two or three handsome, urn-shaped blooms of a deep crimson.

I named the rose Little Albert, and genuinely mourned when the bush expired in a severe freeze during the following winter. *Ars longa, vita brevis est.*

As I mentioned before, the American Rose Society, in addition to 338 different species of roses, recognizes thousands of named varieties that have developed from a small proportion of these original species. Some of the new varieties have' resulted from chance—or, at least, without human intervention. Sometimes a rose, self-fertilized with its own pollen, will produce from its seeds a new variety that differs markedly from the parent plant. Such a new variety is known as a "mutant," and the process is termed "sexual mutation." Again, it sometimes happens that a single rose cane will bear flowers different from those produced on the other canes. If pieces of this cane are rooted, or buds are taken from it and grafted to an understock, the new variety can be perpetuated. Such a variety is known as a "sport," and the process is termed "vegetative mutation."

No one knows what causes mutants and sports. Whatever the cause, some of the resulting varieties have been very valuable. In one short period of about three years, for example, the rose Peace produced sports later introduced as Chicago Peace, Peaceport, Lucky Piece, and Speaker Sam. How many more mutations of Peace went unobserved is a moot question.

Attempts have been made to induce mutation in roses and other plants by exposing them to stimuli of various sorts, notably atomic radiation. If any new varieties of roses have been so produced, I have not heard of them. I once read an account, however, of a rose grower who claimed to produce sports at will. The source was an old book from England about roses—one of Dean Hole's, if

I'm not mistaken. Anyhow, the writer told about visiting the garden of another rosarian that was full of interesting sports of familiar rose varieties. The owner of the garden claimed that he produced these sports at will by a variation on the usual process of bud grafting. Ordinarily, when a bud is selected for grafting onto the roots of another rose, a mature bud will be taken from the central portion of the branch or cane, a bud that, if left to its own devices, would soon sprout and form a flowering stem. But this gardener deliberately took partly developed buds from far down on the canes, near the base of the plant, buds that might never sprout or might not sprout for a long time. These buds, he claimed, he grafted to a suitable rootstock, whereupon a large proportion of the plants so produced bore flowers that differed dramatically from those of the parent bush. Whether there is any truth in this tale, I do not know. I keep thinking, though, that it might be worth trying.

Chances of Success

Most new roses are produced by hybridizing; that is to say, by the process of fertilizing one rose with the pollen of another and growing the resulting seeds.

Rose hybridizing is an exceedingly chancy business if one's intention is to develop new roses for the market. For a rose to be worth introducing by one of the major nurseries, it must have one or more outstanding characteristics—size, color, fragrance, form, or hardiness—that distinguish it from other roses, and by reason of which it excels. After all, it costs about $50,000 to put a new rose on the market. No company in its right mind would lay out this sort of money unless it was reasonably sure that the rose was sufficiently unusual to warrant the risk. In actual practice, the chances are strongly against the hybridizer, so far as commercial exploitation is concerned. Thus, Jackson & Perkins annually grow about 200,000 seedlings of new crosses, the result of hybridizing. Of these, perhaps five or six will be regarded as good enough to put on the market.

Viewed from this perspective, it hardly seems worth the amateur rosarian's trouble to try to develop new varieties of roses. It has been estimated that the amateur has about one chance in ten thousand of producing a commercially valuable rose. Yet the history of rose growing contains numerous instances of amateurs who have succeeded in this highly competitive game. Pemberton, for example, was an amateur. So, too, was the great French hybridist Charles Mallerin, till he decided to turn professional. A recent case in point is Carl Meyer, an amateur rose hybridist from Cincinnati, whose pink hybrid tea, Portrait, won the All-America award in 1972 and was introduced by Conard-Pyle on the American market. I've seen it, and it's a real beauty.

Actually, I think the calculation of odds is misleading. It is not reasonable to judge the amateur's efforts against the needs of the nursery industry. The amateur has an excellent chance of producing varieties that are beautiful and worth growing, even though they may not be sufficiently unusual to warrant introduction on the rose market. And there is always the chance . . .

How to Hybridize

Before you can undertake hybridization, it is necessary to have some understanding of the sexual anatomy of the rose and of how fertilization takes place.

If you examine a fully open rose, one that is about to drop its petals, you will notice that in the center of the blossom there are several—usually five—erect structures with swollen, rather sticky tips. These are the female parts of the flower, and are known as "stigmas." The stigmas are really hollow tubes, each leading to an ovary in the globular base of the flower. Each ovary contains unfertilized eggs, or "ova."

Surrounding the stigmas in a broad ring are a number of slim, erect structures, each tipped with a little knob covered with pollen. These are the male parts of the flower, called "stamens." If pollen from the stamens falls on one of the stigmas, it will immediately be caught and held by the sticky secretion on the swollen end of the stigma. Similarly, pollen from another rose may be carried to it by a bee or by some other insect, or be blown to it by the wind. In either case, the grain of pollen, stimulated by the moisture of the stigma, will begin growing a long, hairlike appendage that will thrust its way down the tube of the stigma till it reaches and fertilizes one of the ova in the ovary.

Once the fertilization has taken place, the base of the rose will begin to swell and grow into a small apple- or pearlike fruit containing a number of seeds. Each seed, of course, is a fertilized ovum.

This is what takes place naturally in roses. Your object will be to use and control this process to suit your ends.

We will suppose, for the sake of illustration, that you wish to cross Peace with Eclipse, using Peace as the maternal parent, and that you have a bush of each rose in bloom.

Early in the morning, select a bud of Peace that is ready to open later in the day. (You can tell because the sepals, the slim, pointed, green leaflike structures at the base of the bloom, will be pointing downward.) With a pair of eyebrow tweezers, pull off all of the petals, exposing the stamens and stigmas. Pluck off all of the stamens, so that the rose cannot fertilize itself, and tie a plastic bag over the emasculated bloom so that insects cannot pollinate it. Later in the day, or the following morning, the tips of the stigmas will have swollen and become moist. While waiting for this to happen, cut off the stamens from an open bloom of Eclipse and put them in an envelope or in a pill box. Leave them in a warm place till it is time to fertilize the Peace bloom.

When the appearance of the stigmas indicates that the Peace bloom is receptive to pollen, remove the plastic bag and place the Eclipse pollen on the stigmas. Some of the stamens, held in tweezers, can be dabbed on the stigmas, or you can transfer the pollen with a small watercolor brush. You will probably find it helpful to use a magnifying glass to observe all of these operations.

Replace the plastic bag after the bloom has been pollinated and tie a cardboard tag to the stem of the bloom with the notation of the parentage: "Peace × Eclipse." You may also wish to add the date. Traditionally, the maternal parent is named first.

After about a week, you can safely remove the plastic bag. Leave the tag for later identification.

Keep the bush sprayed and well watered. After a few weeks, a plump, rosy hip will be formed. When you are convinced that it is thoroughly ripe, pick it. A ripe hip will be plump and brightly colored, like a tiny apple.

Caring for the Seeds

The seeds can easily be separated from the flesh of the hip. Drop them in a glass of water and throw away the ones that float. Those that sink should be dried off and placed in a small pill bottle on a bit of absorbent cotton. Cap the bottle and stick a label on it saying "Peace ✕ Eclipse," along with the date of hybridizing.

Keep the pill bottle in a warm room for two months, then move it to the refrigerator for another two months. If you prefer, you can skip the warm and cold storage and plant the seeds when they are gathered, but the warm and cold treatment seems to increase the reliability of germination.

Planting the Seed

If you gathered the ripe rose hip in late summer or early fall and then kept the seeds for four months in storage, it will still be too early in the season to plant anything in the open ground, unless you live in a subtropical area. Consequently, the typical rose grower, who lives in a fairly robust climate, will need some sort of cold frame or miniature greenhouse in which to plant his rose seeds.

For most areas a cold frame will provide sufficient frost protection. A suitable frame can easily be built (see Figure 11, page 198). Make a bottomless wooden

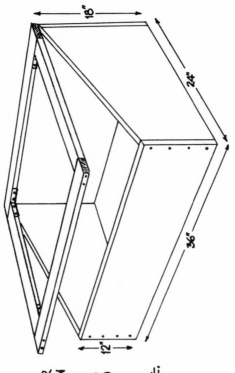

CONSTRUCTION DETAILS:
THIS IS MERELY A BOTTOM-
LESS BOX WITH A HINGED
LID, TO BE COVERED WITH
CLEAR PLASTIC. IT IS
BEST MADE OF 3/4" EXTERIOR
FIR PLYWOOD, BUT COMMON
LUMBER WILL DO. DIMEN-
SIONS ARE NOT ABSOLUTE,
BUT THIS SIZE WILL HOLD
AN ASTONISHING NUMBER
OF PLANTS AND IS SMALL
ENOUGH FOR EASY STORAGE.
PAINT LIBERALLY.

R.A.B.

FIGURE 11.
SIMPLE COLD FRAME.

box with the sides cut on a slant, like the walls of a shed, and cover it with an old window sash; or construct a top with a wooden frame, like that of a window screen, and cover it with clear plastic such as is used as a substitute for storm windows. In either case, fix it so that the cover won't blow off in a high wind, but can be propped open on particularly warm days. A cold frame of the dimensions shown in Figure 11 can be used to raise an astonishing number of plants from seed. Set it up flat on the ground in full sun, and put a couple of inches of sand inside to provide drainage. Flats or flower pots can be set directly on the sand.

You will need suitable potting soil. I suggest equal parts of good garden soil, sand, and peat moss. Add a tablespoon of bone meal for each quart of potting mixture and shake it all together in a paper bag. Make up a lot and save the excess soil for use later.

Whether you use a flat or a large flower pot makes little difference. Fill it with soil, level it, and plant the seeds an inch apart and a quarter inch deep. If the seeds from more than one cross are being planted in the same container, plant them in rows and label each row with the necessary information on a tongue depressor or plant-marker stick set upright at the end of the row. *Don't trust your memory.*

An alternate way of starting your seeds is to plant them indoors in some sort of miniature greenhouse. Commercial greenhouses of this sort are available from several manufacturers. They usually consist of a plastic base and a domed transparent cover. Some models have heating wires in the base. All are small enough to go on a table in front of a window. Personally, I prefer to use them under fluorescent light, keeping the light about a foot above the cover and letting it burn about fifteen hours a day.

An effective device can be improvised out of a tin loaf pan, some coat-hanger wire, and a little clear plastic (see Figure 12, page 201). Make wire end hoops to fit the width of the loaf pan and to stick up about six inches. Punch some holes in the sides of the pan for drainage. Fill it with earth and plant the seeds in it. Then insert the hoops in the soil, drape transparent plastic over the hoops, and fasten it around the sides of the pan with a tightly tied string or a very large rubber band. Water it by setting the whole shebang down in the sink in an inch or so of water until the soil can soak up a good load of moisture. Then place the device in a cake pan or cookie sheet that will hold water.

Examine the plastic covering regularly. If it stays so beaded with moisture that you can't see though it, cut a few slits in the sides and top with a razor blade, to allow for a little exchange of air.

Whether you place your seeds outdoors in a cold frame or indoors in some sort of miniature greenhouse, there is some danger of a white mold—called "damp-off" —forming on the soil and killing the little seedlings. To avoid this, it is well to dust the soil lightly with a good rose fungicide, such as Captan, Maneb, or Phaltan.

Excessive heat will hinder rather than help germination. A temperature of 55° to 60° F. is about right, if you have any way of controlling the temperature, as with air conditioning. If you are raising the plants under artificial light indoors, a basement or an unheated garage will often be found most suitable so far as temperature is concerned.

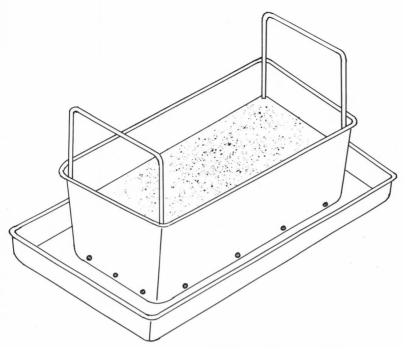

CONSTRUCTION DETAILS:
PUNCH DRAIN HOLES IN LOAF PAN.
FILL WITH SOIL MIXTURE. MAKE
HOOPS TO SUPPORT PLASTIC FROM
WIRE COAT HANGER. SET LOAF PAN
IN CAKE PAN OR COOKIE SHEET.
DRAPE PLASTIC OVER HOOPS AND
SECURE BELOW RIM OF LOAF PAN
WITH STRING OR RUBBER BAND.
PLACE IN SUNNY WINDOW OR
UNDER 40-WATT FLUORESCENT LAMP.

FIGURE 12.
MINIATURE GREENHOUSE FOR STARTING SEEDS.

R.A.B.

Handling the Seedlings

If you are lucky, some of the seeds will begin germinating two or three weeks after they are planted. The first leaves to be produced will be two little rounded things, quite unlike the three- or five-leaflet compound leaves of roses. After a week or so, true leaves of this sort will begin to appear above the first two. Wait till the seedling shows two or three sets of leaves. Then take it up most gently—a table fork makes a good digging tool—and transplant it into a two-inch unglazed clay pot containing some of the soil mixture left over from that in which the seeds were planted (page 199). *Don't use a different soil.* Keep the little potted rose in a sheltered place where it will get plenty of sunshine. Be sure the soil is moist but not wet. If the weather is still cold, with danger of frost, keep the plant either in the cold frame or in a cool room under fluorescent light. If it is kept indoors, set the pot on some fine gravel in a shallow dish and keep water in the bottom of the dish, to provide a humid atmosphere around the little seedling.

You will probably find it desirable to transplant the seedling to a four-inch pot when it gets about six inches tall. By this time, the weather may be warm enough to allow you to set the pot outdoors, buried or "plunged" to its rim in the soil of the rose bed. Give it some shade till it can get used to the change.

Moving the seedling from a small pot to a larger one calls for considerable care. First fill the larger pot with soil, about a quarter full. Then upend the pot containing the seedling and tap the bottom smartly with the heel of your hand. The seedling should come out with the whole ball of earth and roots unbroken. (You will soon learn how to place your left hand over the flower pot with the stem of the plant coming up between the second and third fingers; thus, when the root-ball comes free of the pot, the seedling will drop into your hand, instead of onto the floor.) Settle the root-ball in the soil in the larger pot, adjusting for depth as may be needed, and then fill around the sides of the root-ball with more soil. A pencil makes an excellent tool for tamping the earth down in the pot.

The seedling will usually have its first bloom when it is still ridiculously small. You won't be able to tell much about your new rose from this first bloom, except for the color and fragrance. The blooms borne by the mature plant may have a different number of petals and may be shaped quite differently from this first bloom, which is usually unimpressive.

When the seedling gets to be about a foot tall, it will have outgrown the four-inch pot. You will now be faced with making a decision: whether to plant the seedling in the rose bed and let it take its chances, or to re-plant it in a still larger pot. I would consider repotting only if I felt it essential to keep the seedling in shelter during the winter to come. In mild-climate areas I see no reason for *not* setting the seedling out in the rose bed and many impelling reasons for doing so, not the least important being that, for best performance, the bush needs unobstructed room for its roots.

Precautions Against Loss

Assuming that your efforts at hybridizing have been successful and that you have one seedling plant that means a great deal to you, how can you assure that you won't lose the plant and the new variety along with it through accident or freezing weather?

In the first place, you can take cuttings as the seedling grows and root them under constant mist. This will improve your chances simply by giving you more plants to work with.

You can take buds and graft them to a suitable rootstock, such as multiflora, Dr. Huey, or Ragged Robin. Actually, it is very desirable to do this, since it may materially affect the performance of the variety. Under the stimulus of a different and very vigorous root system, the rose may produce finer blooms in larger quantities.

Finally, you can take cuttings in the fall and root them under glass during the winter.

The original plant, and any new ones produced, can be wrapped in straw against winter freezing and soil can be hilled up around the base of the plant. With forethought you should be able to multiply your stock to a point where the danger of losing the variety is minimal.

Planning Your Hybridizing

Your chances of producing desirable new roses will be considerably improved through intelligent planning. Random crossing of whatever roses are handy *might* produce what you want in a rose, but the likelihood is slim.

You may have been exposed during a course in biology or botany to Mendel's laws of heredity, by means of which it is possible to predict with some accuracy the characteristics of a hybrid. Unfortunately, Mendel's theories apply best to pure-bred stock and won't work very well with garden roses, whose ancestry is hopelessly mixed up and mongrelized. There are, however, some useful rules of thumb in rose hybridizing.

First, you are likely to get a particular characteristic in a hybrid if both parents display it. If you look up the parentage of most red roses, for example, you will usually find that a preponderance of the ancestors on both sides were red. On the other hand, Charlotte Armstrong, a light red or deep pink rose, resulted from crossing clear yellow Soeur Thérèse with deep red Crimson Glory.

If you are aiming at producing a yellow rose, for example, you would do well to cross two outstanding yellow roses, perhaps King's Ransom and Golden Masterpiece, or Eclipse and Mrs. P. S. Du Pont. If you want a blend, you might try crossing two blends, such as Peace and Lady Elgin or President Herbert Hoover and Granada.

Another good bet is to repeat some of the crosses that have already produced fine roses. Thus you might try Charlotte Armstrong × Peace, the cross that produced Garden Party. While it is wholly unlikely that you would get Garden Party again, there is a good chance that you would get another fine rose.

Out of curiosity, I went through *Modern Roses 6* * to see just how feasible it was for the average rose grower to repeat some of the crosses that have resulted in splendid new roses. Here are some crosses and the resulting new variety:

* The most authoritative source of information on the parentage of roses is the following book: *Modern Roses 6* (Harrisburg, Pa.: The McFarland Co., 1965).

Parents *	Offspring
Circus × Queen Elizabeth	Camelot
Soeur Thérèse × Crimson Glory	Charlotte Armstrong
Charlotte Armstrong × Mirandy	Chrysler Imperial
Charlotte Armstrong × Montezuma	Grand Slam
Tiffany × Cavalcade	Granada
Masquerade × Peace	Grand Opera
Golden Masterpiece × Lydia	King's Ransom
Chrysler Imperial × Charles Mallerin	Oklahoma
Queen Elizabeth × Blanche Mallerin	Mount Shasta
Peace × Sutter's Gold	Personality
Virgo × Peace	Royal Highness
Chrysler Imperial × New Yorker	American Home
Pinocchio × Crimson Glory	Fashion and Vogue
Goldilocks × Fashion	Peach Glow
Masquerade × Fashion	Woburn Abbey

As you will see, none of the parent roses shown above is rare or unusual, although in American gardens some are more commonly grown than others.

Any search of the pedigrees of modern roses will disclose that some roses appear over and over again with startling frequency. Consequently, the amateur rose hybridist would do well to grow some or all of these key roses. I would suggest the following varieties:

* The first rose named is the maternal parent in each cross.

Hybrid Teas and Grandifloras	*Floribundas*
Charlotte Armstrong	Garnette
Crimson Glory	Spartan
Queen Elizabeth	Pinocchio
Peace	Fashion
Eclipse or Golden Masterpiece	
Blanche Mallerin	

Using Your Resources Fully

You would be better off to repeat the same cross with several blooms than to make the cross only once. Thus, if you decide to cross Peace with Crimson Glory, you would do well to fertilize several Peace buds with Crimson Glory pollen. In this way you will get a large number of seeds, and your chances of producing a winner will be considerably increased.

It is helpful, also, to make your crosses two ways. When you emasculate the Peace blooms, you may save the stamens and use them to pollinate some Crimson Glory buds. Again, you increase your chances of success.

Some roses have been particularly successful as maternal parents: Peace, Charlotte Armstrong, and Crimson Glory in particular. You might set up a breeding program with one or more of these varieties as the maternal parent and use a different pollen on each bloom fertilized.

Record Keeping

All rose breeders keep a record of their experiments in what is usually referred to as a "stud book." A typical entry will record the names of both parents and the date, and usually a key number will be assigned to each cross that will henceforth be used to describe the cross and any progeny that result. These key numbers are usually coded, that is, one can interpret them if he knows how. For example: 012-70. This might stand for the twelfth in a series of crosses made in 1970. This system, you will observe, would allow for 999 separate crosses in one year.

Should it happen that you are so fortunate as to develop a commercially valuable rose, this precise sort of information about the rose's ancestry will be crucial to your success in interesting a nursery in introducing your rose.

APPENDIXES
AND
INDEX

Name and Plant Patent Number if protected	Breeder	U.S. introducer & year	Bush	Bloom form	Bloom color	Bloom size	Fragrance	Remarks
Americana PP 2058	Boerner	Jackson & Perkins 1961	medium	double	deep red	large	strong	One of the most luminous of all red roses
American Heritage* PP 2687	Lammerts	Germain's, 1965	medium	double	ivory & salmon	large	nil	Color varies with weather and locale
Apollo* PP 3322	Armstrong	Armstrong, 1972	tall	double	yellow	large	nil	Very showy and free blooming
Aquarius* PP 3128	Armstrong	Armstrong, 1971	medium	double	pink blend	large	nil	Good exhibition rose
Arlene Francis PP 1684	Boerner	Jackson & Perkins, 1957	medium	double	yellow	large	strong	
Big Red PP 2693	Meilland	Conard-Pyle, 1967	very tall	double	deep red	very large	nil	One of the largest blooms of its color
Blanche Mallerin Pat. Exp.	Mallerin	Conard-Pyle, 1941	medium	double	white	large	medium	One of the most perfectly formed white hybrid teas. Very free...blooming
Buccaneer Gr. Pat. Exp.	Swim	Armstrong, 1952	tall	double	light yellow	medium	medium	Very vigorous and reliable
Camelot* Gr.	Swim & Weeks	Conard-Pyle, 1964	very tall	double	salmon-pink	large	slight	Very vigorous, free blooming; hardy
Candy Stripe PP 2278 (sport of Pink Peace)	McCummings	Conard-Pyle, 1964	very tall	double	pink with white stripes	very large	strong	Similar to Pink Peace except for stripes. Lovely and different
Century Two PP 3340	Armstrong	Armstrong, 1972	medium	double	deep pink blend	very large	strong	Rather like Charlotte Armstrong, but larger
Charlotte Armstrong* Pat. Exp.	Lammerts	Armstrong, 1940	tall	double	dark pink or light red	large	strong	A fine reliable rose of great vigor and refinement; very generous

Name and Plant Patent Number if protected	Breeder	U.S. introducer & year	Bush	Bloom form	Bloom color	Bloom size	Fragrance	Remarks
Chicago Peace PP 2037 (sport of Peace)	Johnson	Conard-Pyle, 1962	medium	double	pink-gold blend	very large	nil	Blooms more highly colored than those of Peace
Christian Dior* PP 1943	Meilland	Conard-Pyle, 1961	very tall	double	deep red	very large	faint	Exhibitionform; great vigor; generous
Chrysler Imperial Pat. Exp.	Lammerts	Germain's, 1952	tall	double	deep red	large	strong	One of the finest deep red hybrid teas; very generous. Unusually fine form
Colorama PP 2862	Meilland	Conard-Pyle, 1969	tall	double	pink-gold blend	large	light	Very bright and decorative. Blooms loosely cupped when fully open
Columbus Queen PP 2170	Armstrong & Swim	Armstrong, 1962	medium	double	2-tone pink	large	light	Vigorous and generous. Blooms show fine form
Comanche* Gr. PP 2855	Swim & Weeks	Conard-Pyle, 1969	tall	double	orange-red blend	medium	nil	Very vigorous and generous
Command Performance* PP 3063	Lindquist	Howard Roses 1971	tall	double	orange	medium	light	Very good bloom form; generous bloom
Condesa de Sastago	Dot	Conard-Pyle, 1932	medium	double	red & gold bicolor	large	light	Very free blooming; vigorous
Confidence Pat. Exp.	Meilland	Conard-Pyle, 1953	medium	double	pink blend	large	medium	Especially lovely form and delicate colors
Crimson Glory Pat. Exp.	Kordes	Jackson & Perkins. 1935	medium	double	deep red	large	strong	One of the great. Its only real fault is that the bush is rather lax
Dainty Bess	Archer	Archer, 1925	medium	single	pink	large	nil	Blooms in large clusters; prominent maroon stamens
Day Dream PP 3077	Armstrong	Armstrong, 1969	tall	double	pink-yellow blend	large	light	Vigorous plant; exhibition form
Eclipse Pat. Exp.	Nicolas	Jackson & Perkins 1935	medium	double	yellow	medium	slight	Still a standard for clear yellow roses. Very reliable

APPENDIX A HYBRID TEAS AND GRANDIFLORAS

Name and Plant Patent Number if protected	Breeder	U.S. introducer & year	Bush	Bloom form	Bloom color	Bloom size	Fragrance	Remarks
Eiffel Tower PP 2332	Armstrong & Swim	Armstrong, 1963	tall	double	pink	large	strong	Glorious buds; fine exhibition rose
El Capitan Gr. PP 1796	Swim	Armstrong, 1959	very tall	double	scarlet	medium	slight	Blooms in small clusters; very generous and vigorous
El Cid PP 3075	Armstrong	Armstrong, 1969	medium	double	orange-red	medium	slight	Unusually generous bloom
Electron* PP 3226	McGredy	Armstrong, 1973	medium	double	dark pink	medium	light	Usually blooms in small clusters; very vigorous
Firelight PP 3078	Kordes	Jackson & Perkins 1971	medium	double	coral	very large	light	Unusually good stems for cutting; fine form; very hardy
First Love Pat. Exp.	Swim	Armstrong, 1951	medium	double	pink	small	slight	Unusually good form
First Prize* PP 2774	Boerner	Jackson & Perkins, 1970	tall	double	pink-cerise blend	large	light	An almost perfect rose for exhibition
Forty-Niner* Pat. Exp.	Swim	Armstrong, 1949	medium	double	red & gold bicolor	medium	slight	Very striking
Fragrant Cloud PP 2574	Tantau	Jackson & Perkins, 1968	medium	double	coral to red-orange	large	strong	A handsome rose of fine form; very showy
Garden Party* PP 1814	Swim	Armstrong, 1959	tall	double	white-edged pink	large	slight	A nearly white rose, highly reliable and extremely prolific. One of the great
Garden State PP 2349	Meilland	Conard-Pyle, 1964	tall	double	deep pink	large	light	Vigorous; very generous
Golden Gate PP 3060	Warriner	Jackson & Perkins, 1972	medium	double	yellow	large	light	Blooms hold color well in hot weather

Name and Plant Patent Number if protected	Breeder	U.S. introducer & year	Bush	Bloom form	Bloom color	Bloom size	Fragrance	Remarks
Golden Girl Gr. PP 1912	Meilland	Conard-Pyle, 1959	tall	double	yellow	large	slight	Blooms more freely than any yellow rose I have grown. Very reliable
Golden Prince PP 2949	Meilland	Conard-Pyle, 1969	medium	double	yellow-orange tinged	large	light	Blooms singly or in clusters. Orange tinge is distinctive.
Granada* PP 2214	Lindquist	Howard, 1963	tall	double	red-gold blend	large	slight	Abundant bloom; very vigorous and healthy
Grand Slam PP 2187	Armstrong & Swim	Armstrong, 1963	tall	double	medium red	large	medium	Generous bloom
Gypsy* PP 3163	Weeks	Conard-Pyle, 1973	tall	double	orange-red	large	light	Very heavy bloom; quite distinctive color
Heirloom PP 3234	Warriner	Jackson & Perkins, 1972	medium tall	double	lilac	medium	strong	Distinctive and lovely. Very free blooming; very vigorous
Helen Traubel* Pat. Exp.	Swim	Armstrong, 1951	medium	double	pink blend	large	slight	Very handsome, but may show weak neck
Indiana PP 2597	Meilland	Conard-Pyle, 1965	tall	double	bright red	large	slight	Free blooming; hardy and vigorous
Irish Gold PP 2769	Dickson	Jackson & Perkins, 1970	short	double	yellow-pink blend	medium	nil	Exhibition form; good show rose. Very hardy
John F. Kennedy PP 2441	Boerner	Jackson & Perkins, 1965	medium	double	white	large	light	Vigorous growth, but color often shows very faint greenish tinge. Form unusually good
John S. Armstrong Gr. PP 2056	Swim	Armstrong, 1961	tall	double	very deep red	medium	nil	One of the blackest of all deep crimson roses. Very generous
Kaiserin Auguste Victoria (K.A. Victoria)	Lambert	not recorded; 1891	medium	very double	white	medium	strong	An old stand-by, still holding her own
King's Ransom PP 2103	Morey	Jackson & Perkins, 1961	medium	double	dark yellow	large	slight	More free blooming than many yellow roses. Very fine bloom form

Name and Plant Patent Number if protected	Breeder	U.S. introducer & year	Bush	Bloom form	Bloom color	Bloom size	Fragrance	Remarks
Lady Elgin PP 1469	Meilland	Conard-Pyle, 1957	tall	double	orange-apricot blend	large	medium	Wholly exquisite but demanding care. True exhibition quality.
Lady X PP 2691	Meilland	Conard-Pyle, 1967	tall	double	pale lavender-pink	medium	slight	Very vigorous
Laura PP 2986	Meilland	Conard-Pyle, 1970	medium	double	salmon-pink	large	medium	A nice rose, named for Mrs. Sidney Hutton, Sr., a great and much loved lady
Lemon Spice PP 2836	Swim & Armstrong	Armstrong, 1966	medium	double	pale yellow	medium	strong citrus	The perfume is wholly distinctive, like Lemon Verbena
Lotthe Gunthart PP 2585	Armstrong	Armstrong, 1964	tall	very double	deep red	large	nil	Blooms resemble red peonies; very free blooming and vigorous
Lowell Thomas Pat. Exp.	Mallerin	Conard-Pyle, 1943	medium	double	yellow	medium	nil	Blooms freely
Lucky Lady* Gr. PP 2829	Swim & Armstrong	Armstrong, 1967	tall	double	two-tone pink	medium	slight	Very free bloom
Lucky Piece PP 1948 (sport of Peace)	Gordon	Wyant, 1962	tall	double	orange-red blend	large	slight	Has the qualities of Peace, differing only in color
Marie Antoinette PP 2928	Armstrong	Armstrong, 1968	tall	double	pink	large	slight	Generous bloom
Medallion* PP 2997	Warriner	Jackson & Perkins, 1973	tall	double	apricot-pink blend	very large	light	Great beauty of form; unusual vigor, and freedom of bloom
Mirandy* Pat. Exp.	Lammerts	Armstrong, 1945	tall	double	deep red	large	strong	Still among the top roses of its color

Name and Plant Patent Number if protected	Breeder	U.S. introducer & year	Bush	Bloom form	Bloom color	Bloom size	Fragrance	Remarks
Miss All-American Beauty* PP 2625	Meilland	Conard-Pyle, 1968	medium	double	deep pink	very large	medium	One of the most exquisite of the pinks. Fine vigor
Mister Lincoln PP 2370	Swim & Weeks	Conard-Pyle, 1964	very tall	double	deep red	very large	strong	In my opinion, the best red hybrid tea on the market. Very hardy and free blooming
Mojave* Pat. Exp.	Swim	Armstrong, 1954	medium	double	orange blend	large	medium	An excellent, free-blooming rose
Montezuma Gr. Pat. Exp.	Swim	Armstrong, 1955	tall	double	orange	large	nil	Very free blooming and vigorous
New Yorker Pat. Exp.	Boerner	Jackson & Perkins, 1947	medium	double	bright red	large	slight	Reliable, tough, and generous
Nocturne* Pat. Exp.	Swim	Armstrong, 1947	medium	double	deep red	medium	slight	Another fine old variety, hard to beat
Oklahoma PP 2326	Swim & Weeks	Weeks, 1964	medium	double	very deep red	large	strong	A real beauty, different and generous
Oldtimer PP 2999	Kordes	Jackson & Perkins, 1971	medium	double	apricot-gold blend	very large	light	An unusually handsome blend, excellent for cutting
Olé Gr. PP 2474	Armstrong	Armstrong, 1964	medium	double	vermilion	medium	nil	Blooms reminiscent of carnations; distinctive and free blooming
Pascali* PP 2592	Lens	Armstrong, 1969	tall	double	white	medium	nil	Beautiful form, fine for cutting
Peace Pat. Exp.	Meilland	Conard-Pyle, 1945	tall	double	yellow-pink blend	very large	nil	Perhaps the greatest rose of all time
Perfume Delight PP 3282	Weeks	Conard-Pyle, 1974	tall	double	pink	large	strong	A handsome rose, fine for cutting
Pharaoh PP 2859	Meilland	Conard-Pyle, 1970	tall	double	two-tone red	large	light	A very different rose, scarlet flushed with maroon. Fine for cutting
Pilgrim PP 3132	Armstrong	Armstrong, 1970-1971	tall	double	bright red	large	medium	Distinctive red-veined leaves

APPENDIX A   HYBRID TEAS AND GRANDIFLORAS

Name and Plant Patent Number if protected	Breeder	U.S. introducer & year	Bush	Bloom form	Bloom color	Bloom size	Fragrance	Remarks
Pink Peace PP 1759	Meilland	Conard-Pyle, 1959	very tall	very double	dusty pink	very large	strong	To me, the finest pink yet developed; has every desirable quality
Polynesian Sunset Gr. PP 2530	Boerner	Jackson & Perkins, 1965	tall	very double	coral-orange	very large	light	An unusually vigorous plant, very distinctive and generous
Portrait* PP 3097	Meyer	Conard-Pyle, 1972	tall	double	deep pink	large	strong	An excellent, vigorous rose, fine for cutting
Proud Land PP 2737	Morey	Jackson & Perkins, 1969	tall	very double	red	large	strong	An unusually vigorous, reliable rose, fine for cutting
Queen Elizabeth* Gr. Pat. Exp.	Lammerts	Germain's, 1954	tall	double	orchid-pink	large	medium	The first of the grandifloras, and still holding its own; very free blooming
Red Chief PP 2927	Armstrong	Armstrong, 1967-1968	tall	double	red	very large	strong	Vigorous, fine for cutting
Roundelay Gr. Pat. Exp.	Swim	Armstrong, 1954	medium	double	red	large	medium	Unusually vigorous
Royal Highness* PP 2032	Swim & Weeks	Conard-Pyle, 1962	medium	double	pale pink	large	strong	Excellent show rose. Protect against thrips
San Antonio Gr. PP 2844	Armstrong	Armstrong, 1967	tall	double	red	medium	nil	Vigorous, good for cutting
San Diego PP 2900	Armstrong	Armstrong, 1969	medium	double	light yellow-pink blend	large	nil	Very attractive form
Scarlet Knight* Gr. PP 2692	Meilland	Conard-Pyle, 1968	tall	double	dark red	medium	light	Very vigorous; good for cutting
Seventh Heaven PP 2832	Swim & Armstrong	Armstrong, 1966	tall	double	wine-red	large	strong	Unusual color, good form

Name and Plant Patent Number if protected	Breeder	U.S. introducer & year	Bush	Bloom form	Bloom color	Bloom size	Fragrance	Remarks
Show Girl Pat. Exp.	Lammerts	Armstrong, 1946	medium	double	pink	large	strong	Very fine show rose. Vigorous growth
Sierra Dawn PP 2914	Armstrong	Armstrong, 1967-1968	medium	double	pink-apricot-yellow blend	large	strong	Good show rose; fine form
Simon Bolivar PP 2705	Armstrong	Armstrong, 1965	medium	double	orange-red	large	nil	Very hardy; resistant to mildew
Smoky PP 2981	Combe	Jackson & Perkins, 1970	medium	double	see remarks	medium	strong	Color varies from orange to plum. A novelty
Soeur Thérèse	Gillot	Conard-Pyle, 1931	medium	double	yellow	medium	slight	Free blooming and vigorous; blooms sometimes flushed with red
Song of Paris PP 2669	Delbard	Armstrong, 1964	medium	double	pale lavender	large	strong	Vigorous and free blooming
South Seas PP 2184	Morey	Jackson & Perkins, 1962	very tall	double	coral-pink	very large	medium	Blooms often exceed 7 inches in diameter; very generous bloom
Starburst Gr.	Meilland	Conard-Pyle, 1970	medium	double	orange-red-yellow blend	medium	light	Very showy; tends to bloom in small clusters
Sterling Silver PP 1433	Fisher	Jackson & Perkins, 1957	short	double	very pale lavender	medium	strong	Bloom form exquisite
Strawberry Blonde Gr. PP 2707	Armstrong	Armstrong, 1965	medium	double	coral-orange	medium	strong	Petals strongly veined with cherry red; charming
Summer Rainbow PP 2746	Jelly	Conard-Pyle, 1967	tall	double	pink-yellow blend	large	slight	Vigorous and free blooming
Summer Sunshine PP 2078	Swim	Armstrong, 1962	tall	double	deep yellow	large	slight	Valuable for its exceptionally bright color.
Sunset Jubilee	Boerner	Jackson & Perkins, 1973	tall	double	pink-yellow-white blend	large	light	Very fine cutting rose

Name and Plant Patent Number if protected	Breeder	U.S. introducer & year	Bush	Bloom form	Bloom color	Bloom size	Fragrance	Remarks
Sutter's Gold Pat. Exp.	Swim	Armstrong, 1950	tall	double	yellow, flushed red	large	strong	One of the few really fragrant yellow roses
Swarthmore PP 2444	Meilland	Conard-Pyle, 1963	tall	double	light red, flushed deep red	large	slight	Unusually long, handsome buds and distinctive coloration
Tiffany* Pat. Exp.	Lindquist	Howard, 1954	tall	double	pink-yellow blend	large	strong	One of the loveliest of pink blends; very easy-going. An ideal show rose
Touch of Venus PP 3131	Armstrong	Armstrong, 1970	medium	very double	ivory-pink blend	medium	strong	Excellent show rose
Tropicana PP 1969	Tantau	Jackson & Perkins, 1962	tall	double	clear orange	large	medium	One of the great roses of all time. Vigorous, hardy, and generous. Nearly perfect form
Valencia PP 2651	Kordes	Jackson & Perkins, 1967	medium	double	apricot-orange	large	light	Very fine form; distinctive color
Vin Rosé PP 3018	Boerner	Jackson & Perkins, 1969	very tall	double	clear pink	medium	light	Very free blooming; excellent for cutting
White Masterpiece PP 2998	Boerner	Jackson & Perkins, 1972	medium	very double	white	very large	strong	Fine form, highly disease resistant; excellent for cutting
World's Fair Salute PP 2558	Morey	Jackson & Perkins, 1964	medium	double	deep red	large	strong	An exceptionally good cutting rose; fine form

Name and Plant Patent Number if protected	Breeder	U.S. introducer & year	Bush	Bloom form	Bloom color	Bloom size	Fragrance	Remarks
Angel Face* PP 2792	Swim & Weeks	Conard-Pyle, 1969	short	double	deep lavender tinged ruby	medium	strong	For me, the *only* lavender floribunda
Apéritif	Boerner	Jackson & Perkins, 1972	medium	double	ivory-pink blend	large	light	Exquisite form, delicate color; free blooming
Apricot Nectar PP 2594	Boerner	Jackson & Perkins, 1965	tall	double	pink-apricot blend	very large	strong	More like a hybrid tea than a floribunda; enchanting and unique
Bahia* PPAF	Lammerts	Armstrong, 1974	low	double	orange blend	medium	light	Low, spreading plant bears very heavily. Very spectacular bloom
Betty Prior Pat. Exp.	Prior	Jackson & Perkins, 1938	very tall	single	dark pink	medium	light	Generous bloom; makes a good hedge
Bon-Bon* PPAF	Warriner	Jackson & Perkins, 1974	medium	double	pink & white bicolor	medium	light	Very good source of color; blooms very freely; distinctly different
Cecile Brunner	Ducher	not recorded 1881	dwarf	double	pink-yellow blend	small	slight	Commonly called the "Sweetheart rose." Properly a polyantha
China Doll Pat. Exp.	Lammerts	Armstrong, 1946	dwarf	double	pink	small	slight	Extremely heavy bloom; fine for edging
Circus Pat. Exp.	Swim	Armstrong, 1956	medium	double	yellow-red blend	medium	slight	No two blooms alike; very colorful
Circus Parade PP 2150 (sport of Circus)	Begonia & De Vor	Armstrong, 1963	medium	double	yellow-red blend	medium	slight	Essentially similar to Circus, but showing more spectacular coloring
Contempo PP 3102	Armstrong	Armstrong, 1970-1971	tall	double	copper orange	medium	nil	Distinctive coloration

FLORIBUNDAS

Name and Plant Patent Number if protected	Breeder	U.S. introducer & year	Bush	Bloom form	Bloom color	Bloom size	Fragrance	Remarks
Europeana* 2540	de Ruiter	Conard-Pyle, 1968	low	double	medium to deep red	medium	nil	Blooms in very large clusters; unusually decorative. Very good show rose
Fabergé PP 2886	Boerner	Jackson & Perkins, 1972	medium	double	pink-yellow blend	large	nil	Blooms of hybrid tea form, many borne singly. Superb for cutting
Fashion* Pat. Exp.	Boerner	Jackson & Perkins, 1949	medium	double	peach pink	large	slight	One of the great floribundas; exquisite form
Fire King* PP 1758	Meilland	Conard-Pyle, 1959	tall	double	scarlet	medium	slight	Very brilliant color; vigorous and free blooming
Garnette Pat. Exp.	Tantau	Jackson & Perkins, 1951	short	double	deep ruby red	small	slight	Wonderful corsage rose; very free bloom; great substance
Gene Boerner* PP 2885	Boerner	Jackson & Perkins, 1969	tall	double	pink	small	slight	Blooms of perfect form borne very freely
Ginger PP 2293	Boerner	Jackson & Perkins, 1962	tall	double	orange	large	slight	Extremely vigorous and hardy; very generous; distinctive
Gold Cup* PP 1683	Boerner	Jackson & Perkins, 1957	medium	double	yellow	large	slight	One of the best yellow floribundas
Golden Garnette PP 1898	Boerner	Jackson & Perkins, 1960	short	double	yellow	large	strong	Fine bloom form; long-lasting when cut
Ivory Fashion* PP 1686	Boerner	Jackson & Perkins, 1958	medium	semi-double	ivory	large	nil	One of the most exquisite of white roses
Jazz Fest PP 3323	Armstrong	Armstrong, 1971	medium	semi-double	cerise	medium	light	Distinctive in color. Very attractive
Lili Marlene PP 1986	Kordes	Jackson & Perkins, 1961	tall	double	deep cherry red	large	slight	Very vigorous; extremely heavy bloom; striking
Little Darling Pat. Exp.	Duehrsen	Elmer Roses, 1956	short	double	yellow-pink blend	small	slight	Blooms resemble Peace in miniature; exquisite and hardy

Name and Plant Patent Number if protected	Breeder	U.S. introducer & year	Bush	Bloom form	Bloom color	Bloom size	Fragrance	Remarks
Red Gold* PP 3006	Dickson	Jackson & Perkins, 1971	medium tall	double	gold & cerise bicolor	medium	light	Very lovely bloom form; distinctive, very showy color
Red Pinocchio Pat. Exp.	Boerner	Jackson & Perkins, 1947	medium	double	blood red	medium	slight	Another old favorite; tough and generous
Saratoga* PP 2299	Boerner	Jackson & Perkins, 1963	medium	double	white	large	strong	Lovely form, great vigor. One of the finest whites yet developed
Spanish Sun PP 2809	Boerner	Jackson & Perkins, 1971	short	double	yellow	medium	strong	To my mind, the best yellow floribunda
Spartan Pat. Exp.	Boerner	Jackson & Perkins, 1955	tall	double	orange-red	large	strong	An unusually fine rose, handsome, generous & hardy
Summer Snow Pat. Exp.	Perkins	Jackson & Perkins, 1936	low	double	white	small	nil	Good for low hedges
Sunspot PP 2576	Fisher	Conard-Pyle, 1965	medium	double	yellow	very large	nil	Unusually large blooms of hybrid tea quality; seldom out of bloom
Tamango PP 2857	Meilland	Conard-Pyle, 1971	tall	double	crimson	large	light	Very showy and distinctive
Woburn Abbey PP 2319	Cobley	Jackson & Perkins, 1964	medium	double	orange-red blend	large	slight	Exquisite in form and color; very vigorous and generous
Yellow Cushion PP 2549	Armstrong	Armstrong, 1966	medium	double	yellow	large	light	Very free blooming; good for massing
Zambra PP 2140	Meilland	Conard-Pyle, 1964	short	semi-double	orange & gold bicolor	medium	slight	Unusual; very bright and showy

APPENDIX C CLIMBERS

Name and Plant Patent Number if protected	Breeder	U.S. introducer & year	Bush	Bloom form	Bloom color	Bloom size	Fragrance	Remarks
Blaze Pat. Exp.	Kallay	Jackson & Perkins, 1932	10'	double	scarlet	medium	light	Probably the leading climber. Better strains repeat bloom. Extremely vigorous and showy
Blossomtime Pat. Exp.	O'Neal	Bosley, 1951	6'	hybrid-tea type	2-tone pink	large	strong	Repeats freely
Cl. Big Splash PP 3076	Swim & Armstrong	Armstrong, 1969	6'-8'	cupped double	red-yellow-white blend	large	nil	Different and colorful
Cl. Cadenza PP 2915	Armstrong	Armstrong, 1967	6'	semi-double	red	small	strong	Very free blooming.
Cl. Charlotte Armstrong Pat. Exp.	Morris	Armstrong, 1942	6'					Blooms same as bush form; see Appendix A
Cl. Chrysler Imperial PP 1582	Begonia	Germain's, 1957	6'					Blooms same as bush form; see Appendix A
Cl. Circus PP 2074	House	Armstrong, 1961	6'-8'					Blooms same as bush form; see Appendix B
Cl. City of York Pat. Exp.	Tantau	Conard-Pyle, 1945	8'-10'	semi-double	ivory	medium	strong	Blooms only in early summer. Very hardy, profuse bloom, rampant. To my mind, the best white climber
Cl. Crimson Glory Pat. Exp.	not recorded	Jackson & Perkins, 1946	8'-12'					Bloom same as bush form; see Appendix A
Cl. Peace Pat. Exp.	Brady	Conard-Pyle, 1950	8'-10'					Bloom same as bush form; see Appendix A
Cl. Spartan PP 1616	Martinez	Jackson & Perkins, 1964	5'-7'					Bloom same as bush form; see Appendix B
Cl. Sutter's Gold	Weeks	Armstrong, 1950	6'-8'					Bloom same as bush form; see Appendix A
Cl. White Dawn	Langley	Univ. of Minnesota, 1949	8'-10'	hybrid-tea form	white-blend	medium	light	Vigorous, recurrent, very hardy

Name and Plant Patent Number if protected	Breeder	U.S. introducer & year	Bush	Bloom form	Bloom color	Bloom size	Fragrance	Remarks
Cl. Tropicana PP 2701 see Appendix A	Boerner	Jackson & Perkins, 1971	6'-8'	....				.....Blooms same as bush form;
Delbard's Orange Climber	Chabert	Armstrong, 1968	6'		orange	medium	nil	Different and free blooming
Don Juan PP 1864	Malandrone	Jackson & Perkins, 1958	8'-10'	hybrid-tea form	dark red	large	strong	Free, recurrent bloom; one of the very best
Golden Showers* PP 1557	Lammerts	Germain's, 1956	6'-8'	hybrid-tea form	yellow	large	light	Best in cool weather; lovely in bud; stands without support
High Noon* Pat. Exp.	Lammerts	Armstrong, 1946	6'-8'	hybrid-tea form	yellow	medium	light	Recurrent bloom; may show red blush; stands without support
Kassel	Kordes	not recorded, 1957	6'-8'	hybrid-tea form	burnt orange	medium	light	Generous, recurrent bloom; will stand without support; said not to be reliably hardy in cold climates
Paul's Scarlet Climber	Paul	not recorded, 1961	6'-8'	semi-double flat	scarlet	medium	slight	Not recurrent, but superb when in bloom
Rhonda PP 2854	Lissemore	Conard-Pyle, 1969	6'-8'	hybrid-tea form	coral-pink blend	large	nil	Strongly recurrent; excellent for cutting
Royal Gold PP 1849	Morey	Jackson & Perkins, 1957	5'-7'	hybrid-tea form	yellow	large	light	Recurrent bloom; a fine pillar rose

Name and Plant Patent Number if protected	Breeder	U.S. introducer & year	Bush	Bloom form	Bloom color	Bloom size	Fragrance	Remarks
Baby Darling PP 2682	Moore	Sequoia, 1964	tall	open	apricot	1¼"	some	Excellent plant and color
Baby Gold Star	Dot	Conard-Pyle, 1940	medium	double	yellow	medium	some	Gold yellow
Beauty Secret	Moore	Sequoia, 1965	medium	H.T. form	red	1¼"	sweet	Excellent color, form, and keeping quality
Bo-Peep	deVink	Conard-Pyle, 1950	medium	star-shaped	blush pink	small	none	Good for cutting
Chipper PP 2764	House of Meilland	Conard-Pyle 1966	tall	full double	coral-pink	medium	none	Good vigor
Cinderella	deVink	Conard-Pyle, 1953	low	double flat	white	1"	none	A classic
Climbing Jackie	Moore	Sequoia, 1957	climber	full	ivory	1¼"	sweet	Climbs to 5 feet
Crimson Gem NEW	deRuiter	Conard-Pyle, 1974	medium	full	red	1"	none	Excellent
Debbie PP 2911	Moore	Sequoia, 1966	tall	full	yellow blend	1¼"	some	Like a tiny Peace
Desert Charm PPAF	Moore	Sequoia, 1973	medium	full	deep red	1¼"	nil	Flower long lasting; resists heat
Easter Morning PP 2177	Moore	Sequoia, 1960	medium	H. T. form	ivory	1¼"	sweet	Abundant bloom
Eleanor PP 2175	Moore	Sequoia, 1960	tall	high center	pink	1¼"	apple	Good plant
Fairy Moss PP 3083	Moore	Sequoia, 1970	medium	open	pink	1½"	nil	Abundant bloom
Fiesta Gold PP 3331	Moore	Sequoia, 1970	medium	flat	yellow	1¼"	some	Excellent plant
Fire Princess PP 3084	Moore	Sequoia, 1969	tall	flat	orange red	1½"	nil	Bright color; long lasting blooms
Gold Coin PP 2921	Moore	Sequoia Nurs. 1967	low	double	yellow	1"	some	Blooms well
Green Ice PPRR	Moore	Sequoia, 1971	medium	flat	green white	1¼"	nil	Shows more green tint when grown in partial shade
Happy Time PPRR	Moore	Sequoia, 1974	climber	full	red & yellow bicolor	1"	some	Climbs to 4 feet